In *Crushing Insecurity*, Dr. Kim
careful, we will suffocate the dre̲

Honest to the core, this book is captivating, gritty, and thought-pro-
voking. Described as mental and emotional fuel, this is a fresh word for
those who long to increase their confidence, explore their creativity, and
stretch into their purpose. Let these words unlock your future.

—Tracey Mitchell, award-winning author
and international speaker

I have known Kim Allen for well over 20 years, in the capacity as my
small group leader, then as a member of our Discipleship Group, sub-
sequently as a Discipleship group leader of multiple long-term groups,
teaching and mentoring women, and perhaps most importantly, as a
close friend. I have seen firsthand the challenges of her life journey and
have seen the transformed life and character she progressively brought to
those challenges. Now Kim transparently and honestly shares her journey with all the attendant struggles and obstacles, and more importantly,
offers a wealth of hard-earned wisdom to guide others to a richer life in
the arenas of faith, family, business, and education.

—Dennis Powell, Senior Texas District Judge

If you're searching for significance, purpose, the ability to be who you
were created to be, and to inspire and motivate others to do the same,
*Crushing Insecurity* is the book for you. Author Kim Allen dives into the
trials, challenges, and obstacles that threaten our confidence and emotional, physical, and spiritual well-being that can hinder the delicate balancing act required in our lives now and to reach our destiny. Be willing
to examine your life and make the necessary behavioral adjustments,
based on Biblical principles, as you take this journey with Kim.

Having worked closely with Kim Allen for ten years at Little Cypress-
Mauriceville CISD, I can assure you she is a well-respected person

of the utmost character and integrity. She served as the Director of Technology, while I was Superintendent and was a vital member of our District Administrative Team. Because of the nature of her job, Kim was involved in every aspect of the District. Besides leading her department, she advised the District. Additionally, she assisted in reviewing the Technology Applications TEKS for Computer Science curriculum and created and presented Professional Development for Faculty, Staff, and Administrators.

—Pauline Hargrove, Ed.D., Educational
Consultant and Retired Superintendent


"Crushing" is spot on in the description of how we must deal with insecurity! Insecurity leads to double mindedness, and you can go nowhere while you are looking everywhere. Dr. Kim Allen brings years of leadership experience to this greatly important subject. Purpose can be paralyzed by insecurity. Dreams can be detoured by insecurity. Destinies can be destroyed by insecurity. Dr. Allen's book is radiation therapy destroying the metastasizing emotion of insecurity. I recommend this book and its principles as one of the most important books you will place in your achievement and success library.

—Dr. Mike Brown, Lead Pastor of Faith and Wisdom Church,
Founder and CEO of Strength and Wisdom Ministries


It has been my honor to have had Kim Allen as an influence in my life for more than 20 years. I first met Kim when applying for a position, and I knew then that she was something unique and special. She took the time to mentor me and taught me not only how to do my job well technically, but the virtues of being kind and compassionate in every interaction I had. I witnessed firsthand Kim's interaction with her husband and family outside of work which gave me a deeper understanding that Kim not only talks about her faith but openly walks her faith. Seeing her interact with care and commitment made me understand that God truly placed her in my path for a reason.

—Patrick Stewart, Chief Information Officer / VP
of Information Technology – Lamar University

Kim is not an acquaintance but a steadfast and loyal friend for 30+ years. Kim's character is unmatched as her priorities are Family and Faith while managing a successful business, mentoring, teaching, and still helping others succeed in both education and bible studies. Her moral traits and her love for God threads through every challenge and success she faces.

—Kaye Sims, Pastor Crystal Beach Community Church

From Survivor, to Overcomer, to Champion! Kim Allen's story represents the Gold, Silver, & Precious Stones, of the Tenacity of Faith, Hope, & Love! Kim's uncanny gifts of perception and discernment have always refreshed and encouraged me, as her Pastor and Friend. I am positive that you will identify with it, as you read this Celebration, of the Triumph of God's Best Plan! Regardless of whether the top concerns of your Life are Marriage, Children, Family, or Career, get ready for a Holy Spirit Download in your heart, and Blueprint for your Mind! Prepare yourself to be led to realize the Optimum fulfillment of your highest Divine Dreams, Purposes, and Desires in every arena of your Life!

—Dr. James David Brown, President of Kingsway
University and Pastor of Eagle Vision Church

# CRUSHING INSECURITY

*Pushing Boundaries*

———— *and* ————

*Pursuing Dreams*

DR. KIM ALLEN, THD

Library of Congress Control Number: 2022920454

Paperback ISBN: 978-1-63797-110-9
Hardcover ISBN: 978-1-63797-109-3
eBook ISBN: 978-63797-111-6

Cover & Interior Design by Typewriter Creative Co.

Printed in India
10 9 8 7 6 5 4 3 2 1

*To my family who gives me love, confidence, and strength every day. You hold the key to my heart.*

# CONTENTS

*Chapter One*

# OVERCOMING OFFENSE

---

THE WINDOWS SHOOK, AND THE DOORFRAME RATTLED AS the storm began to beat against our home.

This wasn't the kind of storm that would rock one to sleep but the kind that made sleep impossible. The storm had made landfall more than once. This time, its fury was creeping along the Texas coast.

My husband and I watched the radar as the wind picked up and the rain fell in full force. Before making landfall, the hurricane slowed to a crawl, and rain bands repeatedly funneled through the area like riptides. Over sixty inches of rain fell in a short span.

Hurricane Harvey destroyed more than 300,000 structures and 500,000 vehicles. It was one of the costliest natural disasters in US history.

Even now, my emotions are set on edge as I remember how courageous our community was in pulling together. It is not often that we take our eyes off ourselves long enough to see what others are walking through. But this type of trauma pulled out the best in the people we knew. Hurting people transformed into heroes, and those who lost much gave the most.

As I stood and stared at the hurricane's destruction, my thoughts drifted to Meredith. Meredith was one of the first to rush in and respond to those in need. She helped rebuild homes and restore lives. Knowing her history makes her an even greater heroine. Until recently, her life wasn't the kind anyone would want to live out. Like the hurricane, her childhood was overshadowed by dark clouds and littered with emotional debris.

Her father, Jack, wasn't a leader or protector, he was more like an absent alcoholic.

Trapped in the trenches of addiction, his words wounded more than they healed, and his wisdom came out more slurred than it sounded. After years of dysfunction, Jack agreed to enter a treatment program for addiction.

If you have watched or helped someone claw their way out of a dark place, you know how complicated the process can be. The risks of restoration do not come with a guarantee. As much as I wish there were, there isn't a contract that promises love for loyalty. Walking her dad through recovery was like crossing a stream lined with slippery stones for Meredith. One false step could endanger them both. That is the way most of life unfolds, one risky step of faith at a time.

On Meredith's wedding day, she held tight to her father's hand as they walked down the aisle. The hand she clung to during his recovery was the hand that would now release her into her future. Whenever she thinks of that memory, she smiles, knowing the reward of loving deeply had been worth the risk of loving unconditionally. In a way she couldn't explain, she knew she would spend her life helping others walk out of shame-filled seasons.

Years later, Meredith was still taking risks and reaching for those whose feet were slipping. As music floated from the coffee shop and into the lobby, Meredith noticed a lady who looked uncomfortable and lost. Seeing no open tables, Meredith introduced herself and invited the lady to share the couch she had reserved in the corner. Looking relieved, the lady said, "Yes. And by the way, my name is Jen … I'm new. My job relocated me to the area."

As they made their way to the couch, Meredith asked for details about her job and why she transferred to the city. Jen rambled off detailed answers and explained this was the first time she had lived away from her hometown. Over the next half hour, they chatted about places they like to eat, things to do in the city, friends, family, and other small talk.

Before they went their separate ways, Meredith wrote her number on a napkin and invited Jen to call or text if she needed anything. It wasn't long before Jen needed someone to help her dig through a dark situation. She reached out to Meredith, and Meredith reached for Jen's hand.

## THE STORMS OF LIFE

Sometimes the storms of life will try to pry us away from people and places we love the most. If we are not mindful, difficult seasons can cause our hearts to grow dim.

If you are anything like me, I'm sure you have had more than one opportunity to take the easy way out and leave complicated people or situations behind. True, it's hard enough to pull our baggage through life without having to haul someone else's emotional luggage too. Even though it can be easier to journey through life alone, it is never as satisfying as experiencing life with someone you love. I enjoy traveling the world, but as much as I would like to imagine myself carefree and crossing buckets off my list, the truth is, I don't want memories with just me in the frame.

Some of our richest relationships will come along the journey because we chose to let go of offense and let in love.

Trust me, shallow friends are easy to find, but long-term relationships require that we stick out situations we would rather run from. Like Meredith, each of us will experience offenses that will open the door for us to push away from the relationship table. When she had the opportunity to run away, she stayed, and her resilience prepared her for helping others out of adversity. Deep wounds could have easily swallowed up her emotions, but she chose the difficult path of unconditional love.

I promise you, relationships are won or lost on that one phrase—decided to stay.

Maybe you are at a crossroads in a relationship that needs mending. I encourage you to take a minute before deciding and see if there is a way to repair the bridge before setting fire to it.

## PROLONGED PAIN

The other day I scanned through an article about things we do unnecessarily. I laughed as I zeroed in on a section about how people spend more time finding a show to binge-watch than actually watching the show.

In much the same way, I cannot count the number of close friends that allowed past pain to keep them in seasons that they had emotionally outgrown. Expectations that our relationships will be like a Hollywood romantic comedy eventually fade, and 60 percent of us stay in bad relationships for years after they expire.

Prolonging pain is like going into surgery and refusing an anesthetic. The wounds get healed, but one endures unnecessary trauma. I admit that simply hearing the word *trauma* can be an emotional trigger.

By definition, a trigger is "a small device that releases a spring or catch and so sets off a mechanism, especially to fire a gun." In a similar way, our mind is wired to react to things we *perceive* as threats. I stress the word perceive because not every danger is real, and occasionally the threats that are inventions of our minds do the most damage.

## THE DANGERS OF SOCIAL MEDIA

Those of us who use social media regularly know there are multiple opportunities to take posts and comments personally. A few weeks ago, it took me longer than it should have to gather my emotions and let loose a comment left on my page.

As I think back, it wasn't the kind of remark that was openly aggressive but rather couched in a passive-aggressive way. The part that sent my emotions spinning was that a close friend posted it. Her words read like she had been waiting a long time to let those thoughts fly across the keyboard as if her finger had grown restless on the trigger. She finally allowed the tension to unload.

I wasn't annoyed that she shared a different perspective, but I was shocked that she brought the issue to a public rather than a private table.

I spent most of the day scrolling through the thread to see who agreed with her. Work went unfinished because of my distraction, and I canceled my afternoon meeting because it is hard to be creative when you feel others are being critical. I was more frustrated with myself than the comments under the meme by the following day. Losing a day to something as minor as a remark made me question my reasoning. Had I overreacted to her words? Was my friend targeting me, or did she feel our relationship was secure enough to honestly share her thoughts?

Maybe she was simply trying to round out the conversation by adding her perspective. Or possibly my post was crafted in a way that had left her feeling like she was the target.

Within a few days, I cycled through a dozen or more scenarios where I started as the victim and ended up the villain. I hadn't just created an emotional episode; I had made an entire season. As I emotionally constructed through this drama's final scene, I noticed that my friend had tagged me in a picture from a vacation we had taken last summer. The caption of the tag was, "It's time to make new memories." I sighed out loud. A week of peace had been stolen, and I was the thief. The hard part was there were no rewards to show for the imagined emotional battle I had created.

## HYPOTHETICALS AND WALLS

It is easy to get caught in the emotional undercurrent of hypothetical situations. If we do not guard our hearts, we risk getting pulled under by imaginary scenarios or, worse, drowning beneath conjured-up doubts. I am not saying that words are not offensive. But the truth is wrong words have been shot my way more times than I can count. This last year has been incredibly challenging. Friends and not-so-friendly people have brought to the table issues that most of us would rather sweep under the table. Discussions about political views, religious beliefs, and family values have created tsunami-sized waves that have crashed into our casual conversations. More than ever, we must keep our hearts clean and our tongues tame.

Last week I pulled a book by John Bevere from my bookshelf. The highlighted words leaped off the page. "No matter what the scenario is, we can divide all offended people into two major categories (1) those who have been treated unjustly, and (2) those who believe they have been treated unjustly." Regardless of our definition of or feelings about offense, we must forgive.

The words challenged me to the core and made me think about the walls I often built around my heart. Maybe you can think of times when you have used a trowel to seal off people who have brought you pain. Creating buffers and boundaries is often necessary and needful but should never emotionally hold us hostage. Because offenses are guaranteed to come our way, we must learn the delicate balance of safeguarding our hearts without imprisoning our destinies.

When I think of role models of forgiveness, my mind immediately drifts to the story of Joseph, who endured numerous injustices. The arrows of disloyalty were not shot by those who didn't know his heart but by those who understood it best. What I find remarkable is that Joseph never permitted bitterness to be a barrier to his destiny. Instead, he had a close-up view of what it was like to be cut off and accused by people who should have protected and promoted him.

On more than one occasion, I had to push my fingers through the text to try and find out how Joseph found a way to forgive those who betrayed his trust.

Looking closely at his actions and reactions, I noticed that he thought more about God's plan than he did his feelings. That is a challenging task for many of us. It is in our nature to fight for our rights, defend our reputation, and demand justice for the wrongs we have suffered.

But what if we were to decide that healing a nation might be more important than healing our wounds? What if we worked on building bridges before we burned them? Or looked at forgiveness as a way to lavish grace and let go of a grudge.

The ancient book of Hebrews has a unique way of tying together *faith* and *forgiveness*. The writer pens the two words together this way. *"See to it that no one falls short of the grace of God and that no bitter root grows up to cause trouble and defile many"* (Hebrews 12:15, NIV).

Notice how bitterness is an unfavorable comparison to grace. If you have ever tried asking God for forgiveness while holding the animosity in your heart toward someone who has wounded you, you understand the power of this verse. Harboring offenses damages our relationship with God and others. Allowing our thoughts and feelings to control our lives is like trying to swim in the pool of grace with anchors of unforgiveness tied around our waist. If we do not cut ourselves free from the weight of this world, we will sink into a sea of sorrows.

## FORGIVENESS AND FAMILY

If we searched through the Bible's pages, we would have trouble finding a family that didn't experience failure.

The Bible was careful to include families with relational rifts that were strong enough to tear nations apart. Stories that highlight family dysfunction weren't placed in God's word to discourage us but to show us how to avoid frustration and failure.

One of the most well-known stories of family drama is recorded in Genesis chapter twenty-five. In a script written for the big screen, the animosity between two brothers begins in their mother's belly. The account reveals the fight for who would be born first was wrestled out in the womb. Although most siblings eventfully scrap, Jacob and Esau were combative from the moment of their creation. If we were to piece together their story, we would find that they tussled over small and great issues.

Perhaps the most memorable conflict was over ownership of the blessings attached to the birthright. The tale is too long and winding to provide the backstory details.

Just know that like any novel with twisted plots and sordid characters, these two brothers filled up pages that would rival the drama of any royal dynasty. In Genesis 27 (NIV) the story tells of how Jacob deceived his blind father into bequeathing the family's blessings to him instead of the legal heir Esau. The plot thickened when Esau threatened to kill his brother, and Jacob fled to another country to live with their uncle.

If you have experienced a fracture within your family, you can imagine the unfolding stress. Add years of separation to the story, and you understand the kind of tension surrounding the scene. After years of being apart, Jacob decides to extend an arm of reconciliation and make restitution for his devious plot of deception.

It is easy to imagine that making the first step toward reunification took a lot of soul searching. Unpacking and owning up to near-fatal mistakes takes a lot of nerve. Making things right with family members takes even more moxie.

Terrified of Esau's reaction, Jacob sent messengers ahead of their arranged meeting. He was stealthy enough not to send them empty-handed. He sent bequeathed gifts as a way of restoring and righting his actions. The beautiful part of the story is that when Esau saw his brother, he ran to meet him even from far away. They embraced each other and wept for the years they had lost. Esau forgave Jacob, and reconciliation redeemed lost time.

Not all family reunions are so beautiful. I could tell you some traumatic tales of how forcing volatile people into the same environment only intensified their hostilities.

The truth is proper restoration can only be achieved when there is equal submission and a desire to draw together what has been pried apart. Unfortunately, it is far too easy to allow something as insignificant as a family disagreement or attack on our character to create long-standing emotional feuds.

Emotional wars aren't usually waged because of minor conflicts but the chaos that erupts after numerous offenses. It is tragic how easily our relationships get off track and ruined over something that could have been squared away seasons ago, like a runaway weed that compromises the beauty of our perfect flower garden.

## AVALANCHES

Not long ago, we visited a ski resort in Montana. After a day of roaming around the small-town shops, we took a gondola ride to the top of the mountain. The cables eased us up the stunning snow-filled slopes. Watching the skiers slosh their way to the base, I noticed a large green patch that didn't blend in with the terrain. Another passenger explained an avalanche had occurred on that spot several weeks before our arrival. As my mind meditated on that thought, I grabbed my phone and Googled the top reasons for avalanches. My fingers flew across my phone not because I found avalanches fascinating but because I didn't want to be a casualty of one.

A quick scan of the sites gave me the details I needed. Avalanches are triggered when an unstable mass of snow breaks away from the slope. Tearing loose, it slides down the mountain and picks up debris as it goes. Gaining momentum, the unstoppable force obliterates everything in its path. As the gondola pulled onto the platform with a nudge, I discovered one last fatal fact. Each year, avalanches take the lives of over 150 people.

As we skied to the bottom of the mountain, my mind lingered on those statistics. As I zigzagged between the trees, it occurred to me that we emotionally experience similar catastrophes when we lose footing and find ourselves in unsettling situations. If you have ever been in a hurry and slid across something usually sturdy, you know what it is like to feel off-balance and uncertain. Likewise, we must be mindful that triggers within relationships can have the same caustic results.

Sometimes a loose patch of ground can shake a sturdy connection to the core and damage everything in its way.

I remember when I was late for an appointment and ran across an icy sidewalk. Within seconds, my feet flailed over my face and I slid down the sidewalk in an awkward, upside-down way. When I finally found my footing, I looked around to see who had been watching. For a split second, everyone seemed concerned, then, seeing I was okay, broke into laughter. Embracing the moment, I took a deep breath, put my arm across my waist, and bowed. More laughter ensued. That day I learned that falling doesn't always mean failure. Sometimes, it is an opportunity to show others how to get back up after an embarrassing tumble.

Pulling back to the story of Jacob and Esau, it is easy to see how failure could have easily wiped out a family. Jacob could have let shame swallow him up, and Esau could have been justified in keeping his young brother at arm's length. Conflict could have guaranteed lifelong chaos, but one party chose to change the narrative, and a family pulled itself out of the pit of pride.

By pushing his ego to the side, Esau made room to reengage his family. In our lives, the choice to forgive is more than a fresh start to forge ahead, it is the opportunity to show others the goodness of God's love. The kind of love that runs open-armed and forgiving into the ones who may have hurt or humiliated us. The type of redemption the world calls crazy, God calls grace.

The healthiest relationships form over time. Trust is more than the surface-level swapping of our successes; it is created when we can strip down and let others see our naked emotions.

I admit, sharing about success is better told on platforms, while darker days are usually shared around campfires. If King David were a modern-day motivational speaker, he would probably use the tale of Goliath more frequently than the saga with Bathsheba.

Sharing our successes is easier because it reinforces our positive attributes. Sharing our failures is significantly more difficult. We protect our backstories like a lioness guards her young. Cubs are born completely helpless; therefore, the lioness must keep them hidden from all predators, including her pride. The lioness protects them with her life and showcases the art of survival.

In the same way, we expect tribal loyalty from those who have walked paths we are yet to trek down. So as we build out our tribes and tighten our circles, we search for those who will help us gain our confidence and grow our courage. My husband's friend, a doctor, says our relationships do more than sharpen our mental health; they also shape our physical bodies.

While browsing the internet, I stumbled across an article in *Northwestern Medicine,* "Five Benefits of Healthy Relationships." Intrigued by the title, I dug through the findings of the theory and found that positive relationships promote better healing, evoke less stress, create healthier behaviors, and develop a greater sense of purpose and longer life. That list reminded me of all the positive attributes that relationships might bring if we nurture them and give them the necessary care.

Each of us brings to the table experiences that frame our relationships. Some of us may face challenges that have the potential to shatter our self-identity. I know from experience that when I perceive something as a blow to my image, I can respond defensively. As much as we would all love for people to view us positively, those expectations can be the source of our undoing.

I had a friend who called after a difficult day at the office. Over the past six months, she worked hard to develop a groundwork presentation on a significant project. After her team had pieced through every in and out of the project timeline, they felt confident making their pitch. However, two grueling days into the demonstration, they were no closer to knowing if their pitch had made progress or if it was falling flat. Frustrated, she questioned if the presentation was a failure and, if so, would it be a fatal blow to her career aspirations. Her questions went from second-guessing her work to doubting her talent and abilities. The conversation was a slippery slope south, one that I knew had to make a sharp turn and get her mind and emotions moving in the right direction.

Left to their own devices, feelings will carry our minds further downstream, past what is normal to what is unhealthy. If we are going to live a healthy life, we must reroute our feelings. That includes moving from fear into confidence and offense to forgiveness. Before we move forward in our journey, I encourage you to take a few moments to meditate on moments when you have had an opportunity to fall out with a friend or end up sideways in a business deal. Consider how those things may have affected your self-image or triggered an unhealthy response. More importantly, were you able to distinguish between an intentional and unintentional offense? If we study our reactions, we can more easily recognize when we are about to step over the line from self-care to self-loathing.

For many years I underestimated the power of relationships. I finally reached the place where I could seek the hurting like Meredith. I also learned to push away selfish ambitions like Jacob and forgive like Esau. I admit, even now, I don't always get things right the first time. But after years of studying God's word and holding myself accountable to friends and mentors, I grab on to pride less and mercy more. I pray that we will extend the measure of grace we have been given moving forward.

It is then we will discover the beautiful rhythm between peace and purpose.

# *Chapter Two*

# BREAK FREE FROM BETRAYAL

═══════════════════════════════

H IS LIPS LIGHTLY PRESSED AGAINST HIS CHEEK (Matthew 26:49, NIV). The crowd may have thought he was greeting his friend, but Jesus knew it was Judas' hollow way of saying goodbye.

The kiss was a sign that his soul had been sold to a different kind of power. Thirty pieces of silver were all it took to turn a disciple into a deserter. After being in the lineup with the elite twelve, the only thing history would remember about Judas was his bitter act of betrayal.

If you have loved someone who betrayed you, then you know it doesn't matter if disloyalty comes in the form of a kiss on the cheek or a knife in the back. The treachery and the trauma are the same.

Last week, while having lunch with friends, the topic of betrayal was brought to the table. One friend described her swipe with injustice as *deception,* another labeled her encounter *infidelity,* and another spoke of it in words unfit to put into this book. Although our stories were different, the common thread of our experiences was a violation of trust.

I would love to tell you disloyalty is unavoidable, but I cannot. I also dislike owning up to the fact that betrayal weaves its way into our lives when we are vulnerable and likely to miss the telltale signs of treachery.

Hollywood understands the power of betrayal. Numerous box office hits anchor themes around that plotline. Lando Calrissian sells his friend Han Solo to a bounty hunter in a favorite film, *The Empire Strikes Back*. In Disney's *The Lion King*, Scar tricked Simba into thinking he was responsible for his father's death. Convinced he was a murderer, Simba fled the kingdom and went into hiding. I won't bore you by listing off more films because I am sure you can pull personal stories of betrayal from your memory.

## THE MARBLE JAR

At the end of a long workday, I curled up on the couch to rest for a few minutes. I picked up Brené Brown's *Daring Greatly* to read a chapter or two before cooking dinner. My eyes locked onto a passage where she used a marble jar metaphor to explain trust and betrayal. Those words seemed to rise off the page as if they were written just for me:

"When we think about betrayal in terms of the marble jar metaphor, most of us think of someone we trust doing something so terrible that it forces us to grab the jar and dump out every single marble. What's the worst betrayal of trust you can think of?"

We've all been there. I have a friend who drops every relationship she has at the first sign of trouble as a gut reaction. Yet, at the same time, she breaks all connections to the relationship leaving a minefield of unanswered questions and confusion. When I thought about the effect of disengagement in relationships, I recognized how our fear of abandonment challenges our faith.

"What can make this covert betrayal so much more dangerous than something like a lie or an affair is that we can't point to the source of our pain—there's no event, no obvious evidence of brokenness. It can feel crazy-making."

When I read that last sentence, "feel crazy-making," I knew exactly what she was describing.

Regardless of why betrayal occurs the punch of disloyalty will leave us struggling to catch our breath. It took some time for me to see that betrayal, in the form of slow disconnection, is every bit as painful as heartache, divorce, jealousy, and greed. When I broke through the barriers of my thinking, I let go of the pain. Gone was the suffering I had carried like a twenty-pound tote full of regrets and unfulfilled dreams. I was able to see that a slow unraveling of a relationship can be worse than a swift stab in the back.

## SLEDGEHAMMERS AND ANCHORS

Walking through the kitchen, I paused to watch co-hosts of a home improvement show take sledgehammers to a wall. With each hammer strike, paint chips and rotten wood flew off the wall and hit the floor. I thought about how liberating it might be to take wild swipes at things we don't like. Not the careful type of planning that goes into remodeling, but the snatch-the-hammer-and-see-how-hard-you-can-hit kind of reaction.

As I watched the wall come down, I thought about the emotional barriers we place between others and ourselves. Usually, those thick walls are load-bearing, supporting memories of past betrayals and future fears.

So even though society has trained us to take things slow when remodeling how we construct our emotions, it is liberating to tear into walls of worry and pull down partitions of pain.

My family took the boat out for a day cruise not long ago. As the sun was setting, the waves increased, and the boat pitched back and forth. Feeling the effects of the swelling waves, we decided to anchor and keep things steady for a while. The problem was that our nautical line was too short, and the anchor could not grab. As a result, the boat was adrift and tossed around by the summer storm with nothing to latch onto. The simple truth is most people do not think about anchors until they are in the middle of a storm. The experience taught us to check the anchor line length before the boat pulls away from the dock.

My friend Jenn was an anchor. It took me getting stuck in some emotional storms to realize that she was the stabilizer when everything else was turbulent. But, as our friendship grew, I learned that she wasn't always so steady. There were times she had drifted far from shore and lost her beacon.

Jenn and Matt were the perfect power couple. Jenn grew up in the Deep South and lived what many would call the *American Dream*. Raised in a home with supportive parents and extended family, she thrived in the small-town environment. Her dream-like life continued when she and Matt moved to the city. They spent weeks familiarizing themselves with the different communities and had fun looking for a new home. Then, one afternoon, they drove through a popular high-end area with the forty-and-under crowd. When Jenn spotted the house, she grabbed Matt's arm and said, "That one is ours." They took down the number on the sign and bought the house later that week.

At first, they spent all of their free time sitting by the pool and enjoying each other's company.

However, they saw each other less for several months as they began their careers. The corporate grind kept them exhausted and overextended. Jenn missed the way Matt made her laugh, and Matt longed for her undivided attention. They could feel their relationship was drifting, but neither knew how to pull things back together. Although they would later regret the decision, Matt hired his friend Kyle to remodel their patio and pool area.

Starting innocently, Jenn and Kyle spent days working side by side while Matt was away. They talked about their extended families, favorite places to visit, their dreams, and topics that landed closer to the heart. Occasionally his hand would brush against hers. At first, they pulled away; as time went on, they let things linger.

Kyle provided the time and attention Jenn missed. In her mind, she wasn't betraying Matt; she was simply enjoying the company of someone who kept her from feeling lonely. A tug of guilt kept Jenn from crossing lines that couldn't be uncrossed. She prayed that God would give her the strength to untangle her emotions and find the courage to communicate her needs with Matt. After talking through their issues, Jenn and Matt decided to make a fresh start after a long night.

Their first step was to make each other a top priority. Like many couples, they were too busy building careers to notice that they were undermining their family. Like pulling dirt from beneath a sandcastle to build a turret, business undermines the foundation and leaves everything unsteady.

## LOST PEACE

Living life at warp speed complicates our communication ability and leaves us looking for lost peace. Years ago, I read *The Busy Persons Guide to the Done List*. In a paradoxical way, I hurriedly scanned through the book to mark it off my summer reading list. As I flipped through the pages, my eyes landed on this bit of information:

"Forty-one percent of to-do lists were never completed." It is also interesting to note that fifty-one percent didn't even make a list.

I read through those words a few times to understand that we often complete tasks even though they are not on our to-do lists. In a culture that applauds multi-tasking, we have become masters at achieving goals—they are simply the wrong goals. Imagine a marksman hitting the center of a target only to discover he or she aimed at the wrong bull's eye. That is exactly what happens when we lose sight of our relationship goals. Our affections and attention often land on the wrong person or plan. Like Jenn and Matt, our hearts are swift to betray us. Marriage shouldn't be an item we cross off our multi-task list but should be engraved on the top of our priority list. Trust me, the simple act of setting aside time for each other can prevent significant heartache.

Society structures time away from relationships and forces us to sink into our careers more than ever. Having spent years in a highly competitive technical field, I understand the stress and pressure of a demanding job. There were days I felt like every ounce of life was sucked out of me, as if I was free-falling from a plane without a parachute.

Other days, I felt the addictive high that comes with success. Between the euphoric highs and lows, emotionally, I was crumbling. I spent countless nights staring at my laptop. Tears would run down my face because I could not find a way to wrap up my work. I would have to develop critical thinking skills and technical design solutions to advance in information technology.

Looking back, I see that God guided me into this field to become a strategic problem solver. At the time, I didn't understand the connection between solving business problems and resolving people's struggles. Sometimes it is easy to miss the subtleties of how God is training us for the next season of our life. Life was going in the right direction; I just didn't understand the map. It was similar to the first time I saw an object printed on a 3D printer. The first few passes of the printer reveal only the foundation. It takes a while for the image to take shape and appear.

## PURPOSEFUL RELATIONSHIP REJUVENATION

After an eighteen-hour day, my husband and I fell into bed and started planning our overdue vacation. As we carved out the details, we arranged things so our kids could stay with our parents over spring break. A month later, we stepped off a plane and felt the chill of the arctic air. Alaska's summertime temperatures hovered in the forties and fell further once the sun dropped behind the mountains.

After gathering our luggage, we boarded a bus to the cruise ship. We slid into seats near the back of the bus and looked out of the large floor-to-ceiling windows. As the bus moved forward, we took in breathtaking landscapes. Waterfalls cascaded over large cliffs, and snow-covered mountains looked like framed artwork. As we rounded a turn, my husband smiled and said, "Look in the sky."

I turned my head in the direction he was pointing and saw an eagle with wings stretched and talons down. Other unforgettable moments happened as the bus weaved across the mountains. For the first time in a long time, we felt the space between us narrow. We looked at each other the way couples do when they know they are keeping betrayal at bay. With our busy schedules, it was time to focus on each other, detach from our professional responsibilities, and just be together. Gene smiled and reached for my hand as we rode silently to the port and boarded the ship. Our journey of reconnection had begun.

## DIVORCE

When Dylan's parents divorced, he felt the fracture of a family splintered by distractions.

Trying to work through the pain, his mom struggled to make ends meet and eventually fell prey to depression. His dad quickly remarried and quietly slipped out of the picture. Dylan's parents were caught up in the chaos of reinventing their lives, and their focus drifted away from him.

As a teenager trying to work through his issues, he fought hard to support both parents, but the truth was his emotions were crumbling, and his heart was hardening. Dylan felt overlooked and forgotten, and without knowing it, he carried those feelings into every future relationship. The only person who hates divorce worse than the child is the parents.

Even though they may have forced themselves to move on, it is still a process of healing for their children and themselves.

After attending a divorce recovery class, my pastor asked me to lead a small group addressing the topic.

I remember looking into the hollow eyes of mothers who felt *parent guilt* because they were spending too many hours away from home. They experienced overwhelming anxiety, torn between providing and being present.

A mother named Kate shared how she had been out of the workforce for years and couldn't pass the tests needed to gain a decent-paying job. My heart sank when I heard her story. I needed to help but wasn't sure how. After praying about her situation, I felt God gave me a strategy to help hurting mothers.

I asked our pastor to let me teach computer skills on Wednesday night. That time would work well for moms who worked during the day and needed free childcare during the class. I knew that my corporate training and my experience as a single mom would be something those women could latch on to.

In a full-circle moment, I felt that my sideswipes with betrayal would make someone's life better. As the word got out, the women came, not one or two, but a classroom full. There was a waiting list the get into the class, which had never happened before.

Leaning in and allowing God to use a painful part of my past was a stretch for my personality. I usually like to keep things tucked away. But a deeper part of me realized that turning tragedy around meant I would have to be transparent. As I opened my heart, the pain that had paralyzed me years ago suddenly had a purpose.

Today, in my study time, the words in Psalm 55:12-14 (NIV) tugged at my heart. Walking through a season of grief, David scribbles out these words about betrayal:

> *If an enemy were insulting me,*
> *I could endure it;*
> *if a foe were rising against me,*
> *I could hide.*
> *But it is you, a man like myself,*
> *my companion, my close friend,*
> *with whom I once enjoyed sweet fellowship*
> *at the house of God,*
> *as we walked about*
> *among the worshipers.*

David is distraught. His language is deafening and loud. Like a wounded animal that a predator has stalked, his words are hauntingly full of hurt. I've not read enough commentary to understand this backstory fully, but from his response, whatever happened cut his heart in half.

If we listed the leaders we know, most share one similar trait: crowds are captivated by their charisma. David had a magnetic personality. People were drawn to his destiny and persuaded by his passion. Maybe that is why he was easily blindsided by betrayal. He was accustomed to people following him; he wasn't familiar with people turning on him.

Maybe we are like David. Then, perhaps, we grow immune to the idea that callous people can carve up our hearts without missing a beat. If you are a loyal friend, then the idea of turning on someone is inconceivable.

A line from the movie, *The Hunger Games* lingers with me, "For there to be betrayal, there would have to have been trust first." The loss of that one word, *trust,* is what snatches away our security. If you have ever had your home or car broken into, you know how hard it is to regain a sense of security.

In the same way, a breach of trust in our relationships can leave our hearts feeling violated and insecure. The assault on our hearts can leave us clamoring to cover our hearts from future intruders.

My friend Kelly was someone who learned to cover her heart.

While working on their graduate project, Kelly's close roommate, Amanda, subtly undermined her role as the project leader. Although Amanda was hardworking and dedicated to her work, she was also full-given to having things her way. When things didn't fall her way, Amanda took a swipe at things until they did.

As an arborist who knows how to bring down a tree, Amanda knew which team members to work on and which way they would fall. Instead of talking things through with Kelly, she worked methodically to undermine her leadership. In a passive-aggressive way, she maneuvered around facts and past the truth. She even deleted data and delayed deadlines. When Kelly found out about the betrayal, she called for a meeting with Amanda. Knowing that her actions put the team at risk, she took away Amanda's access to critical information.

If you have experienced betrayal by a friend, something inside you changes forever. It may be a subtle change or one that creates a bend in your biography forever. Whatever the degree of betrayal, it takes away a particular part of our soul.

That fact doesn't mean that we will be fractured forever; it simply recognizes the truth: Betrayal will make us better or leave us bitter.

When a bone breaks, its structure is altered. Orthopedic surgeons will tell you that the fractured area is unlikely to break again if a broken bone is properly set. If not properly set, the bone will heal but will likely fuse with a deformity. It is held together but in a way that leaves one with diminished strength and loss of motion. Like a broken bone, the act of betrayal requires more than surface-level treatment. I'm not saying that all betrayal qualifies as triage-level trauma, but at the least, we need to make sure the fracture is set in a way that promotes proper healing.

A hurricane devastated our area at the height of my career. I was responsible for restoring communications and IT services at work.

After grueling days with little breaks in between, I slunk into my hotel room at about midnight. As I walked into the living area, I noticed my husband standing on the balcony. When I walked out to meet him, I sensed he had something important to tell me.

Staring blankly, he gave me the devastating news that the damage to the industrial complexes was severe, which meant the company he owned had no way to operate. He softly said, "It's worse than we can imagine. I don't know how my employees will provide for their families."

At that moment, I realized I had put blinders on my emotions. I could see all my work-related stresses with twenty-twenty vision but was oblivious to his needs. Changing my tone, I whispered, "I'm so sorry; why didn't you tell me?"

His words would haunt me, "I don't know … I guess I didn't want to burden you." My phone rang. I ignored it.

Twenty-one days after the hurricane, we returned home. Life changed, and so did my priorities. Our community was like a small war zone. It was hard to imagine that over forty families from our church lost their homes. The once clean and tidy streets were littered with personal belonging that should have been inside, not strewn on the sidewalk. To put it plainly, Main Street looked like a mound at a landfill. Ingrained in my memory is the site my eyes took in as we pulled up to Beth's house.

Spray painted on a piece of ragged sheetrock were the words: "Please don't take our belongings, insurance adjuster coming." The sign knotted up my insides.

I wondered, *What kind of person snatches up someone's belongings during a storm?* I shook my head and walked into the house. The water line was five feet above the floor. The family hoped to salvage a pile of personal things in the next room. Instead, we saw wedding pictures and important papers shoved in a dresser drawer. I bit my lip as my eyes filled with tears. Witnessing the after-effects of the hurricane changed my perspective. I thought of all the hours I had spent at the office, and now all I wanted was time with my family.

Storms have a way of reordering our priorities.

## WHEN THE STORM ARRIVES

I feel a crisp wind blowing across my patio as I write these words to you. It isn't the kind of gust that precedes a storm but the kind that comes when seasons change. In a reassuring way, it reminds me that storms do not last forever. Over time, the pain subsides, grief gives way to hope, and even the riptides of betrayal reverse.

Before we push forward into a new chapter, I invite you to take a moment and reflect on how betrayal has shaped your story. Maybe, like Kelly, you had a close friend betray your trust. Or perhaps the pages of your story read more like Simba's saga; someone shamed you for something you didn't do. Or could it be that like Kyle or Jenn, you were the one guilty of betrayal? However betrayal has affected your life, I am sure it has left a scar or two.

Oddly, when I look at scars, I don't view them as traces of trauma. Instead, I see them as signs of survival. Perhaps that is a healthy way to think of betrayal as a roadmap that leads to redemption. If we are determined to push past the pain to a place of forgiveness, we can rebuild trust. We will then see that our need for intimacy far outweighs our need to insulate our hearts.

# Chapter Three

# TRANSPARENCY

I'M NOT SURE WHAT FILMS YOU ENJOY MOST, BUT I AM SURE you have a list of big-screen favorites. Maybe your box office list includes plots that pull you into a faraway land, a feel-good romance, or a dark-side thriller.

In our home, we are hooked on superhero movies, especially *Fantastic Four.*

One of my favorite fictional characters is Sue Storm, a.k.a. The Invisible Woman. If you haven't seen the movie, I'll be careful not to give the ending away. Just know that Susan went through a storm that changed her life forever. After being exposed to high levels of cosmic radiation, Susan had dual superhero powers. She could bend light waves, make herself and other objects invisible, and create semi-visible force fields to safeguard her environment. I know that sounds complicated. It is, and so was she.

As I watched, then scanned through the film again, I was fascinated by Susan's strength.

What I didn't anticipate was a subtle phrase buried within the storyline. In one part of the story, Susan stopped and said, "I want to be seen and heard."

When I heard those words, I pressed the pause button on my remote. I listened again to make sure I heard the line correctly. I had. The phrase spoke volumes.

I thought of how much courage it took for her to recognize and give voice to her needs. For the first time, I was able to push past her strengths and see her wounded soul. Although Susan could be invisible, that didn't mean she was invincible.

If you have seen a live Broadway play, you understand. Sometimes, the spotlight only blinds those standing on the stage. It is hard to identify as a superhero when you are a trauma survivor.

INVISIBLE

I think there are times when we all feel invisible. It would be hard to tell you about all of my conversations with well-known people who feel *unseen.*

Even people with large followings share their desire for intimacy that isn't tethered to a video feed or tied to a social media site.

Like Susan, most people are weary of wandering around with emotional forcefields set in place. They crave authentic relationships that will give them the courage to lower their emotional guard and let others see their softer side. Over the past few years, I've tried to be the type of friend who recognizes when someone needs me to lean in and listen. I've found that silence isn't always a sign that someone has nothing to say.

Sometimes silent screams and a long pause can mean *I've been through too much to put it into words.*

Verbalizing our vulnerability is not something strong women do well.

Maybe you have a friend like Susan Storm, or perhaps you are a version of her. A combination of strength and weakness. A mixed bag of force and fear. Someone who wants people close but holds them at arm's length. Part superhero, another part that has trouble putting your feelings into coherent phrases.

Trust me when I tell you that you are not the only one who is cut out that way. Some of the strongest women I know hold their emotional cards close to their chests. It's not that they don't want to be transparent; they do. They want to be seen, loved, and heard, not because of what they do but for who they are.

The heart of every hurting person wants to know, will you love me even when I come across as unloving? Are you cheering for me because you need something from me or because you believe in me? Will you find me interesting once I slip out of my superhero cape and into something made for humans?

Getting to that level of authenticity in relationships takes time. It takes a certain kind of courage to let yourself ask the hard questions and to hear gut-level reactions. But courage is the difference between relationships that bring healing and relationships that end up hurting.

MUDDIED VISION

While typing out a social media post, I thought hard about whether I would like those words in ten years.

Like a paper journal, social media has a way of capturing our current thoughts and beliefs; the difference is social media puts it out for the world to see. The topics we once debated face to face are now argued out on Twitter, Facebook, and Instagram. I admit it is easier to hold our ground and fight for our convictions when looking at a screen and not into someone's eyes. The lure of looking at life through an online lens can muddy our vision and make us see things that aren't there.

If you have ever watched the documentary *Catfish,* then you know how easy it is to get sucked into relationships that are not real.

This week, someone told me about a friend who bought an airline ticket and flew across the country to meet someone who falsified their identity. They were shocked when the truth replaced the lies. Another friend told me about a woman in a long-term online relationship with a man who claimed to be single. Thankfully she followed her intuition and cross-checked his identity. He was married and had three small children.

I know that sounds extreme and that most of our social media exchanges don't lead us into dark places. But we must be careful that our emotions do not get hung up on what we see when staring at a screen.

My friend Emily works so many hours that she has *mom guilt* from not spending enough time with her children. You would never know that about her by looking at her Instagram feed. Maybe in a reverse psychological way, she over-posts about her children to keep her feelings at bay. I have a younger friend who throws all her feelings out on social media.

The *like* and *comment* buttons are hip-hinged to her identity. Over coffee, she admitted her compulsion to keep up with her online image had sabotaged her real-life relationships. Like many, the pressure to make a good impression on strangers left little energy for those sitting at her table.

## SYMBIOTIC RELATIONSHIPS

Recently I stumbled across an interesting article that talked about symbiotic relationships.

In case you are wondering, *symbiotic* simply means cooperative or reciprocal. The article highlighted several symbiotic relationships, including the one that exists between crocodiles and plover birds. When I scrolled down through the page and saw a bird sitting in a crocodile's mouth, I was sure the delicate fowl would be reduced to feathers. Expecting the worst, I breathed a sigh of relief when I read that plover birds fly into the crocodile's mouth on purpose.

I know it's odd, but the birds feed on the decomposing meat stuck in the crocodile's teeth. The plover gets a meal for flossing the crocodile's teeth in a twisted yet mutually giving way.

Most relationships struggle to find the delicate balance of emotional equity. Who would land on top of your list, and why if you ranked your relationships in order of importance? What are the core qualities of those who gain the gold medal and land in your inner circle?

Years ago, I had a friend who, without reason, suddenly bailed on our ten-year friendship. I tried to retrace how the fallout occurred but kept coming away without answers. I finally realized that a lack of conflict was the only thing that made that relationship different from others.

We had *zero* friction—ten years without negative words or an argument. As I reflect on that now, I understand that our relationship had grown long but not deep. Authentic relationships will encounter bumps in the road. More than likely, there will be many chances for one or the other to grow bitter before things get better.

But if we are to enjoy the richest part of our relationships, we have to bring the hard questions to the table. We are accountable to not only ask them but to answer them. Being accountable is not easy, but it draws us closer and makes us stronger. One of my favorite scripture verses says it this way, *"As iron sharpens iron, so one person sharpens another"* (Proverbs 27:17, NIV).

## SHINING LIKE DIAMONDS

Mark is the go-to friend who always seems to have what others need. I've also noticed he has a handful of quirky traits. He is the type of guy that pulls out a pocketknife and sharpens it in the middle of a conversation. While I find that archaic, my husband thinks it is practical. I've watched him enough to know that when the blade becomes dull, it must grind across the stone to be made sharp. The friction between the stone and blade polishes and refines both. In the same way, relationships are designed to make us sharper.

If all of our relationships are easy, they will eventually grow dull.

When the word transparency comes to mind, I immediately think about diamonds. I know that sounds shallow, but it's the truth. While shopping online, I clicked on a link about the world's largest gemstones. While browsing around, I discovered that the world's largest uncut emerald, approximately 1,759 carats, is housed in Columbia. If cut and sold, its estimated value is 500 million dollars.

Another link revealed that diamonds are formed under extreme heat and gravitational pressure. Diamonds, the hardest known substance, can only be cut by another diamond or diamond dust. The gem sparkles, and light is transmitted through the stone when crafted by an artisan. The brilliance of the diamond is the reflection of the internal and external white light.

Similarly, we are like diamonds.

The pressures of life and the fire of our experiences make us valuable. When we authentically engage with others, we illuminate truth and allow others to see into our lives. The fact is no one wants to walk around with a dull-looking diamond.

Diamonds are crafted to shine, and so are we. To shine, we have to strip away anything that clouds our luster or darkens our gleam. It requires a great deal of humility to live transparent lives, but that kind of sincerity is what makes us strong and durable.

EXPOSED

Standing on the balcony, David stared at the curves of her body. She was bathing, and her beauty captivated him (2 Samuel 11:12, NIV).

As a married man, he knew he should look away, but his eyes refused to follow his conscience. In a way that kings do, he sent one of his servants to find out who she was. Even though they explained she was Bathsheba, the wife of one of his soldiers, he sent for her anyway.

If you have read this story before, you know where his actions lead—the plot whirls around a heated affair, unplanned pregnancy, and a messy murder. By the end of the story, you have to wonder if *fame* helped turn David, the shepherd boy, into David, the corrupt king.

In a full-circle kind of showdown, Nathan the prophet asked for a meeting with David. When the door clicked shut, Nathan opened the conversation with a story. Telling a winding tale, Nathan vividly described how a wealthy man used his power to take a poor man's lamb.

By the time he was finished talking, David's face was red from fury. He slammed his hand down on the table in a self-righteous gesture and demanded justice for the innocent man. Then, drawing close to David, Nathan pointed his finger at David's chest and said, *"You are the man! This is what the Lord, the God of Israel, says: 'I anointed you king over Israel, and I delivered you from the hand of Saul."* (2 Samuel 12:7, NIV).

Horror fell over David's heart, and he dropped to his knees. The anger David felt toward the wealthy man was now directed at himself. Like David, most of us can remember when we caught a glimpse of the stripped-down version of who we are.

Not the online version, the corporate version, or the red carpet version. But the naked, exposed, and honest account of who we are when no one is looking. When we can get comfortable with that version of ourselves, our lives will flourish.

### THE POWER OF SHARING STORIES

I was surprised when a shy woman in the back of the room raised her hand and asked to share her story.

Erin described the car accident that took her parent's life in a gentle, low-key way. She explained that her father drove through a thunderstorm on the way home from the grocery store and lost control of the car.

Erin's mom died instantly, and several days later, her father passed away. Listening to her words, one could sense that it took courage to share that experience in public. Even though it may have been hard, her words flowed through the room like a tidal wave. Words of strength, faith, and hope washed across the heart of everyone listening.

Through my tears, I scanned the room and saw the same reaction in every person. No eyes were dry and no heart was untouched. Like a cork pulled loose from the bottle, Erin's words set us free in ways we had not expected.

When she let go of her pain, we let go of our chains. We have all fought battles we are not comfortable sharing. Some of our stories may be too painful or shameful. Trust me, admitting our failure isn't easy, but *what if* our stories could help rescue another sister? What if hearing how we have stumbled helps secure someone else's steps? Or sharing about our wrong turns keeps someone on the right path.

That's the kind of person we need in our inner circle; that is who we need to become. The one who will rise up to help others run forward.

### FRAMING OUR WORDS WELL

I've found that words are more harmful than good if they aren't well-framed. I have a friend whose daughter has a hard time filtering her thoughts. Although she means well, her comments come across as *raw.*

Over lunch, Amy and I talked about Heather's say-what-you-feel approach to life. Heather had funneled through numerous job interviews but seemed to have difficulty landing a position. Although she had a great work ethic, she was very open with her thoughts and feelings.

Amy went on to tell me about an interview Heather had at a local clothing store. Squinting at me, she asked, "What do you think about that?" I paused for a few seconds and tried to script my words.

Amy started laughing. "I know. I thought the same thing," she said. "Can you imagine her helping a customer? I can see it now; the customer tries on a dress she loves and asks her opinion. Her response would probably be, 'Wouldn't you like something more age-appropriate?'" We laughed and agreed that sales probably wasn't her best job opportunity. Learning to guard our words can be the difference between success and failure. Holding our peace can also hold open the gate to our destiny. Although we want to weigh our words, we don't want to disguise them completely.

## FILTERS

Flipping through Instagram, I noticed one of our favorite destination spots was tagged on someone else's feed. Weirdly, the pictures were nothing like I remembered. Grabbing my phone, I compared my pictures with theirs. The location was the same, but they captured the moment using a dramatic filter. While filters can enhance the scenery, over-filtering may give off false impressions. Sometimes, we over-filter our thoughts or experiences as a way of self-protection. We may leave out intimate details of our story or hide things that make us look bad. If we constantly filter out the things we don't like, our relationships can become less transparent and more transactional. With technological innovation, our world is growing more transactional by the day.

Our relationships can become routine if we are unwilling to open up and build lasting relationships with others. Deep-rooted friends go the distance and have the unique ability to make us feel at home and secure and, sometimes, slightly vulnerable.

I stood in the museum and gazed at the colorful paintings and photographs. The views of space exploration were magnificent, and I felt a tinge of pride knowing my Uncle Dan's work was on display.

My uncle was a talented artist whose abilities went far beyond drawing or painting. Creativity flowed through his veins. As a teenager, I watched him disappear into his art studio in the early morning hours and emerge at dusk with a canvas slathered in vibrant colors.

Magically, he could take the images in his mind and give them life. It was hard to guess which masterpiece he would create next. Dan was a confident free spirit who wasn't bound to traditional thinking. He wasn't content to color outside the lines; he erased the lines. Growing up, I enjoyed visiting him and my Aunt Joan. They were spontaneous and fun. We enjoyed great conversations, went to exciting places, and embraced life in a relaxed way. Through them, I learned the art of living without pretension.

Stained glass is one of my favorite types of art. It is the perfect combination of beauty and transparency. I love touring historic buildings and studying the colors and patterns of large window panels. The transparent panes allow images of the outside world to filter into the dark interior crevices.

Metaphorically, we should live open lives and draw light into dim places.

## TEARING DOWN OUR WALLS

Melanie stood on the balcony and looked out at the aquamarine water. The sun was shining so brightly that she could see the vibrant blue and yellow fish swimming near the island. On impulse, Melanie decided to take a trip to the island alone. A quick vacation seemed like a good idea. Running from the pain of a broken relationship was behavior she had perfected. She needed someone to talk to that would understand and help her refocus.

Instead, she found herself alone and desperate to uncover the reason her relationship unraveled.

Melanie loved Chris but felt compelled to end the relationship. Last week he was the love of her life; this week, she was alone. Feeling like a failure, she wondered why this kept happening. When she noticed her reflection in the mirror, she didn't recognize the person staring back at her. Angry at herself, she thought, *What is wrong with you? You had a wonderful man who loved you and understood you. Why are you doing this?* Sliding onto the couch, she began to cry. She felt herself spiraling into self-destructive behavior.

Melanie was good at stuffing her emotions at the bottom of her soul. Without realizing it, she alienated the people she loved most. A latchkey kid of successful parents, she was left alone with her emotions ... she didn't know how to make those emotions run. She learned to rely on herself at an early age but desperately sought love and attention. Instead, she felt broken, disconnected, and unlovable. In a word, she was lonely.

As a child, she secretly pulled the covers over her head at night and cried. As the tears flowed, she struggled to comprehend why no one understood her. She wanted someone to notice and accept her. Instead, the thick layers of emotions muted the voice she hid from others. Melanie knew what was needed but didn't have the emotional strength to follow through and find healing.

Living a transparent life requires that we tear down walls of pride and replace them with windows of grace.

Before we begin a teardown, we should ask ourselves whether to completely demolish a structure or just open up the space and make more room for light. Foundations can be repaired, walls expanded, and structures stabilized instead of being reduced to a burn pile.

Similar to a new foundation, when we support each other, the seed of love and acceptance begins to flourish. How can we build authentic relationships without a commitment to open and honest communications?

Sharing our innermost thoughts isn't easy but allows us to expand our minds and souls.

All things considered, we don't always feel we deserve to be understood or accepted. So why do we settle for what we have instead of the great things we are destined to accomplish? Trent Shelton, a former professional football player and president of a Christian-based non-profit organization, produces a two-minute video series called "It's Rehab Time." Please take a few minutes to read this and let it soak in, and encourage you.

"You deserve someone who respects you enough to never lie to your heart. You deserve someone who would still be there for you even when everyone else has walked away. You deserve something that's REAL. Never settle for less." — Trent Shelton

*Chapter Four*

# IMPACT AND EMPOWERMENT

T HE CIVIC CENTER WAS FULL OF ENERGY AS EXHIBITORS, participants, and presenters gathered to kick off the Education and Technology Conference.

On the ride up the escalator, Katie scanned the conference program and realized she needed to rearrange her schedule. Finding an open spot in the hallway was impossible, so she stepped into the auditorium to gather her thoughts. Scanning the room, Katie found an aisle seat in the back row and plopped down.

While she studied the color-coded map, a loud round of applause broke her concentration. Startled, she looked up toward the stage. The spotlight followed a woman walking toward the microphone as the house lights dimmed. Squinting to be sure, Katie thought, *Oh my goodness, that's Reshma Saujani.* Katie was a fan of Saujani's TED talk, "Teach Girls Bravery Not Perfection," which had amassed over four million views.

Reshma began her session by talking about her desire to disrupt the status quo. In a personal way, she shared about running for Congress in New York. She admitted that she was thirty-three years old before she did anything brave because she had been raised to avoid risk and failure.

Katie moved to the edge of her chair and listened as Reshma talked about the small percentage of women in Congress and STEM (Science, Technology, Engineering, and Math) careers. Reshma explained, "Of the 600,000 available Technology jobs in the U.S., women were underrepresented, with only twenty-six percent of computing jobs." Reshma encouraged the women in the crowd to grow comfortable with being uncomfortable and to learn something new.

Those words lingered with Katie, and she shared them with friends over dinner. Adding to the conversation, Kristin shared about an eleven-year-old girl in the United Kingdom who runs a coding club for girls who are passionate about technology. Others shared similar stores of young women working on the front lines in their fields.

When I imagine young world changers, my mind thinks of the young girl whose work will impact future generations. Without her and others like her, the newest form of communication may go undiscovered. I found an interesting video on YouTube showing the potential impact of "missing code" and the role of women in technology. I encourage you to take a moment and think about the thousands of women who have bravely entered the work field in spaces that traditionally came with gender limitations.

Women like Reshma Saujani continue to inspire and make space for future generations of aspiring leaders, artists, humanitarians, politicians, and techies. If you want to look her up, Reshma is the founder and CEO of Girls Who Code, an international nonprofit organization working to close the gender gap in technology. She is also the New York Times bestselling author of *Girls Who Code: Learn to Code and Change the World* and received Forbes' 2012 Most Powerful Women Changing the World.

When I read about women who run full force toward opportunities, I feel inspired to push my self-made limitations out of the way. I know that stepping out and away from the familiar can be frightening. But with each step, we retrain our brains to bypass our insecurities and move forward in faith.

In the same way that a heart bypass redirects blood around a blocked artery, courage diverts our potential away from insecurities and toward opportunity.

## WHY ARE WE AFRAID?

This last week I scanned a blog that highlighted fears and phobias. The list included the usual concerns: snakes, spiders, germs, fear of flying, and fear of tight spaces. But down the list were things I never considered like, *arachibutyrophobia,* which is the fear of peanut butter sticking to the roof of your mouth, or *xanthophobia* fearing the color yellow, or perhaps my favorite *hippopotomonstrosesquippedaliophobia,* which is the fear of long words and in an ironic twist, happens to be the longest word in the dictionary.

As much as we would like to rationalize our fears, sometimes we can't. There are times we have to own the truth: We are afraid of pursuing our dreams because we don't want to risk being disappointed.

Protecting our hearts is something we do well, maybe too well. If we are not careful, we will suffocate the dreams we want to set free. Equally important is balancing our desire to be liked with the leadership plans God has for us. Whether we lead at our jobs, homes, church, or community, we need to refresh our enthusiasm for leading others.

## LIKE ME OR NOT

Not all leaders are likable. Maybe you just thought of one. I did too. If you have a driven personality, you understand that likeability isn't something most of us master overnight. Being an effective and likable leader is a rare combination, a skill set that can take years to develop. My friend Angela, a master communicator, is a likable leader.

As I observed her approach to leading teams, I noticed she went out of her way to make others feel at ease. It was essential to her that other team members felt affirmed and free to share their opinions, even if they were different than hers. Unlike other leaders, she led from behind, giving those around her the freedom to forge their way forward with confidence.

One day, after a luncheon, she approached me with a hug and asked, "Can I do anything to help you?"

Feeling that she genuinely wanted to help, I replied, "Actually, yes. Our team would love your input on a video project."

Without hesitation, she said, "Sure, what's it about?" I gave her a brief overview, and we decided on a date to record the video. The following week, our videography team went to her office and staged the set. Stepping into the frame, Angela warmly addressed the staff and the community and explained the project in full detail.

Then, she paused, looked at us, and asked, "Was that okay?"

I stared and said, "Wow, that was incredible. How do you do that? Can you teach me to be that comfortable on camera?"

She laughed and said, "Thank you, I've had lots of practice. God has given each of us unique gifts. I don't understand the intricate details of your job because he hasn't gifted me the way he has you. And Roger has the unique gift of creative design and Kelly in graphic design. If our team is going to succeed, we need a combination of all of our talents."

In a few words, Angela affirmed, motivated, and empowered us. We left her office confident that our project would be successful. If we work with leaders on an ongoing basis, there will be many who rank low on the likeability list and, a few, like Angela, who challenge our perspectives positively.

For more than a decade, we spent hours out of the week watching family members grind out their athletic skills on the soccer field. Our kids loved the game and were relentless competitors. They were only satisfied if their kicks flew past the goalie and into the net.

The love of the sport sparked our interest in the World Cup, and gradually we picked up on the backstories of international players.

Many international athletes face untold danger once they land in the big leagues. At age sixteen, Khalida Popal fell in love with playing soccer. At that time, women's sports were banned in Afghanistan, and stadiums became a location for public executions. Yet, Popal and several of her friends practiced soccer, after hours, behind their high school.

Their team reportedly faced death threats, and bomb scares while forming the group. She told *People* magazine, "People threw garbage and stones at us and warned us that we had to stop playing soccer or they would kill us." But Khalida's team refused to stop playing and instead traveled around and recruited other women to join the soccer league. Even though helicopters landed on the field while they were playing, and bombs exploded just in front of the compound, they kept playing. The team continued to compete in international tournaments and won an exhibition game against NATO's women's team. Khalida eventually fled Kabul but remained an outspoken advocate for women's rights.

Forming a critical relationship with Hummel, Khalida's soccer team developed a version of the Afghan national team's uniform. The new uniform design covered the players' hair, eliminating the need for the players to wear a hijab during games. The uniform was launched on International Women's Day, a strategic move forward to empower women.

Although most of us do not encounter danger daily, many of us face adversity on the road to accomplishing our goals. Sometimes the journey toward success requires finding the strength to walk out our courage or discover ways to stick out a stormy season. Our quest may not need us to dodge sniper fire; sometimes, the burden is learning how to survive the friendly fire.

The biblical story of Esther is legendary (Esther 1-10, NIV). It has the novel kind of drama that would land at the top of the New York Times bestseller list if written in modern times. Esther, an orphan, was thrust into the spotlight when Ahasuerus, the Persian king, sent his troops to find a virgin queen. Esther, of Jewish descent, was selected and was forced to marry King Ahasuerus. In a story that is too long and complex to retell, the king's highest official, Haman, plots to destroy all the Jews living in Persia.

The scheme is rooted in jealousy, involves treason, and a plot to commit murder. In a bold and sacrificial act, Esther revealed her Jewish heritage to the king and begged him to save her people. Before the story ends, Esther becomes an unlikely hero and prevents the genocide of the Jewish people.

Pause and think that story through. *An orphan girl saved a nation.*

## RESCUING OTHERS

Although our story may not read like a best-selling novel, we still have the opportunity to save others. Maybe our mission doesn't include preventing genocide. Still, it may consist of rescuing victims of human trafficking, providing shelter for those living in refugee camps, or supporting racial and gender equality.

What if the king called on us to endanger our lives to liberate others? Would we be willing to risk our reputations, or even our lives, to see others set free? Embedded in the book of Esther is a rather ominous line, *"And who knows whether you have not come to the kingdom for such a time as this?"* (Esther 4:14b, ESV). That destiny-defining question wasn't exclusive to a young queen in 460 B.C. It is a question for women of every century.

For years, I heard older adults say, "It takes a village to raise a child." I never fully understood that phrase until our children became teenagers. It was then we grasped how much help we would need from others in shaping our children.

If you have children or spend time with young family members, you know how good it feels when they succeed and the sinking feeling when they slip up. As pastors, our children grew up feeling like people in the community had higher expectations of them and us. They were right. Some days we felt like we lived in a glasshouse. And there were challenges to knowing others watched us make mistakes, suffer loss, and walk-through grief.

On the plus side, our glasshouse gave us a better view of the world than had we lived behind thick walls without windows. Others watched us, but we trained our children to watch God.

Maybe I am alone in this thought, but wouldn't it be great if we all had at least one superhuman power? I admit, there have been crisis moments when I longed for some power that could make my weakness strong. Maybe I am dreaming, but imagine what it would be like to open our closets and find superhero outfits. By slipping into something with a large *S* sown across our chest, we could bulk up our self-confidence and change the world.

Sometimes it would be nice to have the same naïve approach to life that we had as kids.

## SUPERNATURAL STRENGTH

Recently, I read about the comic book series *Empowered*. The main character is Elisa Megan Powers. The story tells how Elisa found a package that contained a *hyper membrane outfit*. Whenever she put the power suit on, it gave her extraordinary physical abilities. Although the suit gave her self-confidence and empowered her to help others, the suit had a near-fatal flaw. If the suit became damaged, Elisa's power would begin to fade. Even though Elisa's suit fixed itself, the process took a while.

In much the same way, our wounds don't always heal overnight. There isn't a magic fast track to restoring damaged emotions. It takes time to develop courage and keep our confidence from sliding away.

On occasion, superheroes, just like the rest of us, second-guess their decisions and try to keep fear far away. Once Elisa tried to over-compensate for her lack of confidence by wearing armor over the clothes. The problem was that the armor worked against the outfit. Instead of being invincible, she became invisible. How many times do we layer up to self-protect? Often, to cover up our lack of courage, we clothe ourselves with titles, labels, and overtaxed schedules. Instead of being seen as valuable, we come across as superficial.

I am old enough to recognize when I need supernatural strength. On the days when my faith falters, and my wisdom seems foolish, I grab my Bible and search for scriptures that infuse me with God's power. I read those verses aloud, allowing them to clothe me in supernatural strength. A verse that speaks to my soul is found in a letter that Paul wrote to friends in need. He talked about his weakness and how he needed superhuman grace to give him strength. He explained it this way:

> *"[When I asked God to help with my weakness] each time, he said, 'My grace is all you need. My power works best in weakness.' So now I am glad to boast about my weaknesses so that the power of Christ can work through me"* (2 Corinthians 12:9, NLT).

Paul, the great apostle, didn't hide his weakness but exposed it. His transparent approach encouraged other leaders to embrace grace and become perfect, not in themselves, but in Christ's grace.

Leah had been a high school honor student. Once she graduated, she moved from a small town to a metropolitan city. Alone and away from her family, she felt like she was drowning in a sea of uncertainty.

Unable to land her dream job, she was forced to take a job as a food server to make ends meet. Leah reached out to me for student mentoring during this time, and we began to meet for lunch every Tuesday. We talked about her assignments, challenges, and what we could do to get her back on track during our time. Right away, I could tell she was a brilliant student, but she lacked confidence in her abilities.

A few months into the program, Leah applied for and received academic scholarships covering her tuition, books, and residence fees.

The university had granted her a co-op position in the business department. Her progress was incredible, and she slowly began to rebuild her life and relationships. A few months into our regularly scheduled lunch, she bounded in and began chatting about a mid-term assignment.

She said, "For my term paper, I want to focus on someone who is very successful in the corporate world and makes a difference in their company. You know, someone inspiring,"

Immediately, I thought of Mary Barra. I led into the conversation by saying, "Mary Barra was the first female CEO of General Motors. She was fifty-seven and was the highest-grossing leader of the Detroit Big Three automakers."

Leah nodded with interest and asked, "How much was her salary, including benefits?"

I grabbed my phone to look up some quick facts. "According to Google, she earned $22 million, which landed her the number five spot on Forbes' World's 100 Most Powerful Women. She also worked at General Motors as a co-op student inspecting fenders and hoods. That job paid her college tuition."

Leah smiled and said, "Wow. She started in a co-op job and ended up being the CEO of a large company. So, there is hope for me." We laughed and joked that we would settle for half of her salary. That day, I noticed a change in Leah. One woman's success story empowered her to believe she could accomplish her goals. Several years later, she graduated with honors and accepted a position with a well-known software company.

Empowered CEOs can change the world. Mary Barra catapulted General Motors into the tech space, with ideas, like automated driverless technologies and electric-powered cars.

In her first year as CEO, she issued eighty-four safety recalls which involved 30 million cars. Can you imagine the courage it took to execute a full-scale recall? She also testified before the Senate about the nature of the recalls and why it was in the public's best interest, not her company's, to uphold the decision.

One of Barra's most significant accomplishments was developing policies that encouraged workers to report problems when they noticed them, thereby changing the company's culture and validating employees' input. I found it interesting that General Motors is one of only two global businesses with no gender pay gap. Once again, that was a plan pushed forward by Barra.

Although you and I may never run a Fortune 500 company, our level of influence can be as impactful. Each of us can make an impact right where we are. It may be in a small group setting, a volunteer position, running for election in local politics, or being CEO of multiple businesses. Whether we are meeting a college student for lunch or standing on the Senate floor, we shape our culture and each other.

## BECOMING A WORLD CHANGER

Not every world changer has their picture plastered on *People Magazine*. Some live quiet lives, but their life signature is written all over those they touch. Like a beautiful passion flower grows on vines in the forest canopy of the Amazon Rainforest, the stems drop down so they can be where their pollinators live. These flowers touch every part of the rainforest and are used by indigenous tribes for healing ailments of the heart.

Lindsey was like that beautiful passion flower. Gracefully, she reached out to become a vessel of healing to those who were hurting. As a young girl, she was always the first to offer help or advocate for her classmates.

In college, she used her wisdom to solve problems for others and encouraged them to succeed. After she graduated, she married an army officer.

As a military wife, she often endured long periods without her husband. Instead of whining about her situation, she found purpose in mentoring other military wives and formed support teams for those whose spouses were deployed overseas. Driven to help others, Lindsey established addiction recovery programs, led suicide prevention campaigns, worked with homeless veterans, and was a social worker on staff at a large medical center.

Lindsey was more than a sideline cheerleader; she jumped in the trenches of other people's trauma. I cannot tell you the number of times that she held the hand of someone taking their last breath. She wasn't the kind of leader who was interested in climbing the corporate ladder. Lindsey was the leader who became the ladder when others needed to climb out of gut-wrenching circumstances. While her face may never make headlines, it was often the last face others saw before going to Heaven.

## LEADING IN SUBTLE WAYS

Swiping through social media, I noticed a link to an article, "What Animals Tell Us About Female Leadership." Half-annoyed, I clicked on the page that identified eight animal species that exemplify female leadership. According to research, out of the 5,000 mammals studied, only a tiny fraction of females leads their tribes. Researchers looked for things like evading predators, finding food, or resolving conflicts to find female leadership traits. They narrowed the study to eight species: hyenas, killer whales, lions, spotted hyenas, bonobos, lemurs, and elephants.

A unique finding within the study revealed that the herd naturally follows the female elephants. Cynthia Moss, director and founder of Amboseli Trust of Elephants in Kenya, said, "When it comes to elephants, females are born to leadership. In adult female elephants, there is no choice, nor is there any struggle with males for a position. Males live separately and do not serve as leaders among the family groups of elephants."

In the animal kingdom, leadership emerges when cooperative units are formed.

Within families and small groups, females lead in a more subtle way with encouragement and commitment to invest time in others. Most women leaders in the workplace emphasize teamwork and encourage authentic communication.

The power of associations like our friends, social network connections, and work relationships is essential. I can't tell you the number of times I've watched promising young people connect with the right individuals and quickly advance in their careers.

Unfortunately, I've also watched those who chose the wrong associations and endured long periods without advancement. Each of us has leadership responsibilities and is uniquely qualified to accomplish the tasks necessary to succeed. Whether we strive to smash the glass ceiling, empower students, be a shoulder in a time of crisis, or start a worldwide movement, we need courage and confidence.

God placed a vision for our lives within us. Even though our experiences may be unique, we all have the opportunity to make a difference. Although we can't change our experiences, we can choose to learn from them. We may not find the cure for cancer, build our own rocket, or take a trip to space. But we can make connections, build relationships, and be willing to take risks to empower others. So let's put on our superhero capes and get to it!

*Chapter Five*

# DISCOVERING YOUR SIGNIFICANCE

D O YOU EVER FEEL LIKE YOU ARE AT WAR WITH YOUR schedule? I can't tell you the number of sleepless nights I have suffered through thinking about my overstuffed calendar.

It took years to realize my peace wasn't tied to getting my hands on more but loosening my grip on things I'd had for too long.

In a recent blog post, Tony Robbins explored a theory explaining the human drive for fulfillment. He explained, "Everybody has different goals and desires, but we have the same needs."

He linked six fundamental needs to fulfillment: certainty, variety, connection, growth, contribution, and significance. Although we may value these needs differently, they ultimately shape our thoughts and actions and determine whether we succeed or fail. The search for fulfillment and significance leads some to the center of their purpose and others into a pit of self-pity.

## THE SEARCH FOR FULFILLMENT

I had a friend who sacrificed everything to move to Los Angeles to pursue work as an actress. She spent years surviving off tips she made from a part-time job and crashed on friend's couches.

When she turned thirty, she went into an emotional tailspin. Feeling like she wasted a decade pursuing an elusive dream made her hold other ambitions at arm's length.

Maybe you have ambitions that you kicked to the curb because things didn't work out as you hoped. Whether we carve out a place in the corporate world or chase down creative dreams, we long to be known for something we do well. That longing or internal drive is a powerful force.

I have watched headstrong women work that longing to their advantage, and they ended up thriving. On the other hand, I have also walked with women who let ambition get in front of their character, and they ended up in dark places that were hard to climb out of.

How their stories ended can be traced back to their motive in pursuing those dreams. If we are not mindful, it is easy to miss a turn or two and end up far from our intentions.

## REDISCOVERING OUR PURPOSE

Another friend Megan felt led to help single moms in impoverished neighborhoods.

For the first few years, she stayed true to her mission and accomplished great things in the community. As the years slipped by, she became known as the go-to fundraiser for philanthropic projects.

Although she was gifted at managing charitable campaigns, she lost sight of her original vision. Soon she was swept away by the image of being a community leader and felt void of the compassion she once had for the hurting.

Feeling adrift, she resigned from various boards and let loose of scheduled obligations. She went back to volunteering and teaching a group of women on the weekend. Working with the women in a personal way was the reset she needed to regain her passion.

I am sure that most of us wander away from our goals rather than toward them at some point. Fame and fortune are common lures that can turn our honest efforts into selfish ambition. Sometimes, our search for significance gets muddied up in our good intentions. That is understandable.

But when that happens, like Megan, we need to take a step back to rediscover the purpose behind our passion.

## FINDING PURPOSE IN WHO GOD IS

A few years ago, I felt the need to recalibrate a few of my dreams. After a string of challenges at work and home, I felt uncharacteristically out of rhythm with life.

Subtly, I could feel my self-worth diminishing and experienced a disconnection with my identity. Frustrated, I took a couple of days off work to steady my thoughts and anchored my emotions. One morning while reading a devotion, a simple verse from the book of John grabbed my attention: *"But to all who did receive him, who believed in his name, he gave the right to become children of God"* (John 1:12, ESV).

I read through that verse over and over. With each read through those affirming words became stronger and more amplified. I am God's child.

Later that day, I found other scriptures that helped me navigate my internal storm and find peace in Christ.

## TESTS AND GIFTS

In the business world, employers often administer tests like the Myers-Briggs, High5, Enneagram, and Big 5 Personality to learn more about the applicant. The Myers-Briggs defined me as a Visionary Strategist. Big 5 identified me as a Coach, and Enneagram reports said I valued principles and was driven by the motivational need to be good and right.

Ouch, but true.

If you have taken one of these tests, you know that the results can be as shocking as confirming. I admit that I have taken them all. I found a few *blind spots* in my personality and had to make changes before those glaring imperfections caused tremendous grief. I adjusted and am thankful that I was emotionally secure enough to tackle my weaknesses and not just run with my strengths.

Shortly after joining our church, my friend Michelle asked about taking a spiritual gifts test.

Abandoned by her parents, Michelle was placed in the foster care system at an early age. Thankfully, she found a home with a loving family as a teenager. Wanting to find ways to serve the community and church family, she was excited yet apprehensive to take a test that would highlight her natural gifts and talents.

Over dinner, she gently shared her apprehensions. She asked me what would happen if she gave the *wrong answers*. I assured her that there were no *right* or *wrong* answers. I explained that the test was more of an evaluation to see how her gifts could best be used.

After the test, Michelle seemed happy and eager to push the results into my hands. After scanning the findings, I looked up and smiled. Tears were streaming down her face.

She said, "It's like God looked down on me and gathered all the heartache and pain from my life to show me how much He loved me. Without experiencing hurt in my life, I wouldn't be able to help others who are suffering or in need."

Waving her arms around, she asked, "Can you believe my gift is to help heal people who feel lonely and forgotten?"

Crying between breaths, she went on, "That was me. I was lonely and forgotten. I don't understand why my life took the path it did, but God sent me parents who would show me how to love others. This is one of the best days of my life."

Michelle caught a revelation of things that went beyond her spiritual gifts. She learned about the Holy Spirit and how God sewed together a good plan for her life despite her childhood trauma. It became clear that her destiny wasn't held hostage by dysfunction. Instead, the heartache was a highway for someone else's healing.

The type of miracle moment that happened for Michelle isn't reserved for a handful of people. God has a strategic plan for your life. He knows you completely, more thoroughly than any profile test can reveal. Because your Heavenly Father created your spiritual DNA, He can take every part of your history, even the horror-filled moments, and use them to unlock your destiny.

## TIME, TALENT, AND TREASURE

The other day, I scanned through blogs hoping to find information for my friend, Jessica. A half-hour into my research, I came across the article, *Successful to Significant*. The piece began with a quote by Lee Colan, an accomplished organizational psychologist:

> "You don't have to become an industrial baron and make a billion dollars to live a life of significance. All you have to do is share the resources you already have. However insignificant you may think they are, your resources are often of greater value to someone else than they are to you."

The lead-in sparked my curiosity, and I began to contemplate the idea that we forge strong relationship bonds when we give our resources to others. As I pushed through the rest of the article, Lee suggested three things we can freely give to others: Time, talent, and treasure.

Daily, we make volumes of decisions. Each time we commit ourselves to a *yes* response, we automatically close the door to other opportunities. Conversely, declining certain requests will make room on our calendars for future invitations. Think of it this way, every *yes* or *no* is a placeholder of opportunity. I'm sure you are familiar with the term "Time is Money." The other day a mentor pushed that concept further and said, "In reality, time is a commodity without any material value."

That sentence stopped me in my tracks. My insides froze as I began to analyze how I had been investing my greatest commodity.

Eugene Lang, a self-made millionaire, had an epiphany when he stood before a room of African American and Puerto Rican sixth-graders. Lang had grown up in the same seats as these students in Harlem. When his eyes locked on theirs, his soul searched for words that would convince them to stay in school. Weighing each word, he said, "Stay in school. If you do, I'll help pay the college tuition for every one of you." That moment changed the trajectory of the students' lives.

It was a kairos moment, a bend in your story kind of break.

Those few words brought hope into the room. Six years later, close to ninety percent of the class graduated. Lang made good on his promise. He created the *I Have a Dream Foundation,* which has supported similar projects in over fifty cities.

Lang understood the rewards of philanthropy. His legacy was not about what he acquired but what he left behind. Imagine what could happen to our world if we shared and then lived out that noble philosophy. If, like Michelle and Lange, we gave back a portion of our prosperity to those in pain. Suppose we contributed a part of what we would normally keep. What if we sacrificed so others could survive or reached back and not just forward?

Then, maybe, our soul would feel more anchored to purpose.

## WORKING OURSELVES TO DEATH

Kathryn's beauty and success made other young women jealous.

Intelligent and driven, she set her sights on being a physician and married before turning thirty. But the long hours and sleepless nights that came with attending medical school and performing her residency left her mentally and physically exhausted.

Several years into medical school, she felt her stamina slipping away. Some days it took everything she had to trudge down the halls of the hospital and wrap up her rounds. After accidentally mixing up an elderly patient's medicine, Kathryn asked for a weekend break to visit her family. When she arrived at her parent's home, she slept for eighteen hours straight.

Concerned about Kathryn, her mom brought a meal to her room and sat down on the bed beside her. Speaking softly, she said, "Katy girl, you're going to have to take better care of yourself. I know you want to save the world, but if you aren't careful, you are the one we are going to have to save."

Pushing ourselves to the point of exhaustion sets us up for disaster. Like poking a pinhole in a dam, the tiny hole doesn't create immediate damage, but enough pressure will widen the hole into a gap, and the gap into a breech, until the structure breaks, destroying everything in its path.

Sometimes, our effort to be the stabilizing force for others works against us, and woefully, we do more harm than good.

If you feel overwhelmed or like you are about to break apart emotionally, I encourage you to pull aside and rest. Take a day or two to physically recharge and emotionally regroup.

When I feel pulled in too many directions, I grab my things, pull aside and whisper this verse from Philippians 4:7 (ESV) over and over … *"And the peace of God, which surpasses all understanding, will guard your hearts and your minds in Christ Jesus"* until peace comes.

The thing about fatigue is that it magnifies our feelings of being unimportant or invisible.

When I am tired, my emotions tell me that what I am doing isn't effective.

That in the vast scope of the universe, my problems aren't that important. With all the global chaos, it is easy to feel swallowed up by more pressing issues.

## GOD'S FIRST CHOICE

The other day, I visited The Hubble Space Telescope site and learned that the closest spiral galaxy is Andromeda, a galaxy much like our own Milky Way. It is 2.2 million light-years away from us. There are hundreds of billions of galaxies in the universe, and each galaxy can be as large as 200,000 light-years across.

By comparison, our planet occupies the space of a single blue dot. That's all; a dot that is home to 7,891,049,995 people. Staring at that figure can make us pull in our breath and question our significance.

But the truth is that God sees each of us. As a loving parent, He knows every detail of our story and longs to be involved in our daily life. When chaos comes, He doesn't look the other way or focus on someone else. No, He stands by us in the time of trouble. He works by our side and fights through the hard rounds with us. Even when we don't see an immediate change within our circumstances,

God, through His word, assures us that he is working on our behalf. We are visible. We are significant. We are God's first choice.

## POWER OF AFFIRMATION

Affirmation is like music to our soul.

It is the kind of melody we never want to quit playing. Affirmations are powerful because they are statements of truth. Positive words or reactions from others influence the deepest part of our emotions. Maybe that explains why we naturally seek out compliments or positive verbal reinforcement when our feelings are shaken.

They are powerful because they remind us of who we are when

we feel like we've lost our way. Studies have shown that affirmation decreases stress and encourages optimism.

Last year, our team went through a challenging time. Along with stressful work deadlines, each team member was working through personal challenges at home. Recognizing the need to boost morale, I grabbed some index cards and asked everyone to write something positive about other team members.

Before wrapping up the meeting, the affirming words were read aloud. That simple action changed the atmosphere. The usual formal setting became a place of shared empathy and compassion. A few tearful hugs were exchanged, iron-clad personalities softened, and everyone exhaled pent-up emotions.

The intentional action recalibrated our focus and helped us see each other in an empathetic way.

People who affirm others are a gift to the world. Intuitively, they discern the emotional needs of others, and with grace and wisdom, they know exactly what to say.

When I think of those who change the world with their words, my memory lands on John. Even though John transitioned away from his professional career a few years ago, he didn't stop using his God-given talents to help others. Since retiring, he built an alliance to help people who need food, home repairs, and rides to appointments. He remained engaged with the community, looked for opportunities to serve others, and maximized his time in a productive way.

Unlike some men and women his age, he didn't fall into the trap of feeling lost or insignificant. He continued being the resourceful person he had always been. His life was meaningful because he added value to others.

TAPPING INTO SIGNIFICANCE

Elizabeth Blackwell and Lauren Gardner are legends in their field of expertise. Elizabeth Blackwell was the first woman in the United

States to attend medical school and receive a medical degree. When Elizabeth applied to medical schools, she faced the grim reality that most learning institutions were gender-biased. Except Geneva Medical College in New York, every medical school rejected her application based on her gender.

Interestingly, a group of male students pushed for her application to be accepted. Shortly before her graduation, Blackwell's inaugural thesis on typhoid fever was published in the Buffalo Medical Journal. It was also the first medical article published by a female student in the United States.

Lauren Gardner, a Johns Hopkins University professor, was named one of the top 100 global influencers for leading the team that developed a free and open website that allowed tracking the COVID-19 pandemic in near-real-time. The COVID-19 dashboard became the leading source of centralized data on the coronavirus pandemic. Collecting and displaying data from 188 nations allowed the public, governments, and media to visualize the spread of the disease. Lauren and her team found a way to improve the system by recognizing a significant void in the international public health systems for predicting, preventing, and tracking diseases with catastrophic global consequences.

Both Elizabeth and Lauren tapped into significance and used it to change the world positively. Although both faced adversity, they forged ahead and made remarkable changes in their respective fields. Women in today's culture can pull strength from their brave actions to launch into uncharted waters and new frontiers.

The simple truth is: significance is not something we search for and then sit on. It is to be the catalyst that launches us out to help others, and then the world.

Doing things that have the potential to change the world, or at least the world around us sounds daunting. It is easy for our efforts to get swallowed up in a sea of doubt. More than likely each of us has wondered if what we are doing is making a difference. Is the effort worth all the time and energy we are putting forth? Does anyone notice or care? Every few months, I hit the pause button and ask, *Am I making progress or simply marking time?*

## BECOMING BRAVE

Last week, I looked through my bookshelf for a copy of Becoming Brave written by my friend Tracey Mitchell. One of her philosophies is: *A courageous life is not stumbled upon-it is cultivated.* I sat for a few minutes and let the words sink in. I thought hard about what it takes to make a difference. I purposefully considered all the risks and sacrifices one makes to initiate change in a culture that resists change.

In *Becoming Brave,* Mitchell used a biblical example to express the thought that our choices can liberate future generations. I encourage you to read the twenty-sixth and twenty-seventh chapters of Numbers for the full version of the story. This is a rich parenthetical that describes women who are willing to risk their reputations to create space for women's rights.

According to Mitchell, "The turning point in the history of women's rights can be traced back to five audacious sisters who dared to challenge a culture that had been oblivious to their gender's needs. Rereading their story makes me question: Up to that point, had men simply withheld property from women and the women were just *never brave enough* to ask for their inheritance? For generations our gender has been taught that men are our primary oppressors. But with that acknowledgment I must also concede that our timidity and complacency are not *entirely* the fault of men. Before we excuse away our withering dreams, we must ask if we have voraciously fought to shift the trajectory of our culture."

Mitchell made a strong case that by bravely presenting their plight, a handful of women changed the course of their gender forever. Although the story doesn't confirm their decision was a prayerful one, it is probably safe to assume that they sought God's favor before they asked for man's.

The journey to finding and then holding on to significance is both liberating and daunting. The road lends itself to bumps, resets, and complete changes in direction.

## STAYING THE COURSE

Staying the course and not losing sight of our purpose can feel like we are meandering through a labyrinth. The maze looks easy until the hedges obscure our view or the path repeats itself, and we find ourselves back at the opening gate.

I have found that personal growth often looks less like a tidal wave and more like a small ripple ring.

Progress doesn't come with neon signs flashing, "You're doing great, keep going." And contrary to what we have been told, success tends to quiet down our cheering section, not the other way around.

The uncomfortable truth is significance is usually achieved in the day-to-day moments, when we share a conversation with a friend who feels crushed, meet a goal we have been pushing to achieve for months, or courageously stand up for ourselves or others.

The good things in life are seldom free. They require time, energy, resources, and at the least, minimal effort.

Maybe the cost of peace calls for us to put down the latest novel and read our Bible. A job promotion may require us to take challenging college courses. Launching a new business may demand that we take serious financial risks.

When we step forward in faith, we show God that we aren't just wasting time waiting around for something to happen. Our actions reveal that we are willing to put forth effort while expecting positive results.

As we close out this chapter, I want you to know that I am no stranger to struggle. Just like you, I've been through seasons and situations that almost pulled purpose right out of my hands. There is no doubt that struggles can try to snatch away our significance.

That is why we have to be intentional about keeping our focus forward. When we hold onto what makes us unique and lean into our significance, we amplify our opportunities.

I encourage you to find a quiet place where you can think and meditate without distraction. Take your journal and Bible with you. As you pour over God's word, ask Him to show you what step to take next. In my drive to push forward my dreams, prayer often becomes more like a checklist where I talk more and listen less. Maybe you sometimes feel as if you are bringing a to-do list to God. Instead, let's make a new commitment to listen to God's voice and hear His focus for our lives. Only then can we allow Him to recalibrate our dreams, guide us to our destiny, and understand our significance.

*Chapter Six*

# COMMANDING YOUR COURAGE

S OME PEOPLE RUN TOWARD ADVERSITY LIKE AN OLYMPIAN on a gold medal quest. Others are equally courageous, but their stories don't tumble across newsfeeds or headline the tabloids. Sometimes the most courageous people in our culture live across the street or down the hall. And on a rare occasion, we have a front-row seat to their life.

## STRENGTH AND COURAGE

Like most southern families, my parents thought quotes and collo-quialisms were foundational to childrearing. Occasionally, I hear one of those familiar catchphrases ringing in my head. Just last week, I thought of one of my father's favorite sayings, "Get up, dress up, and buckle up for the ride." I'm sure you would have to hear him say that in his slow southern drawl to appreciate the full meaning.

My mother was one of the fearless ones, who was courageous

in public and behind closed doors. I was fortunate that her courage wasn't the kind that got shoved in a corner; no, it was the contagious kind of courage. If you hung out with my mother for more than a few hours, your perspective would shift, and somehow, you would walk taller when you left the room.

Recently my mom passed away. In her thirties, she suffered a significant stroke and remained paralyzed on the right side of her body. She had the unfortunate experience of being medically misdiagnosed and was denied appropriate treatment. Permanent neurological damage meant Mom had to endure years of physical training as she learned how to speak, write, and walk … again.

As a teenager, I went with her to rehabilitation sessions.

Although it's been decades, my memory can still pull up the painful slips and falls and the sounds one makes as one grunts through therapy. Even now, I can picture her gripping metal bars moving one foot, then the other forward, until she could shuffle a short distance without any help.

Although she did eventually walk again, she never fully recovered using the right side of her body. But, with encouragement from friends, she went back to college and received a master's degree in social work. She thrived, received awards as Handicapped Person of the Year, and helped others until she retired.

In later years, unfortunately, she became a victim of COVID-19 and beat it … twice.

One perfect warm and sunny day, we visited my mom at the assisted living facility. Upon arrival, residents were waiting outside in wheelchairs.

I looked at my sister, and tears welled up in our eyes. It was the first time my mom had enjoyed a sunny day outside in over a year. We couldn't get out of our car but were able to stop and tell her how much we loved her.

She smiled, waved, and modeled the inner courage and strength she possessed. As time went by, she grew thin and frail. The morning

Mom passed away was like an unbelievable dream. Needing something to hang my emotions on, I asked God to give me a word that would describe how my mother embraced life—staring out the window, the word strength roared through the silence.

## TEACH THEM TO CARE

Lately, I have spent time figuring out why some people run to confrontation and others run in the opposite direction. In my quest to see what makes a person comfortable with courage, I found a thread of common traits, including value, vision, energy, and character. The more I read about courageous women, the more fascinated I became. Reading through the lives of audacious women, I stumbled upon the story of Angela Ahrendts.

One of six children, Angela developed a strong work ethic at an early age.

Studying in a small storage area under the stairs of her home, she fought to focus on her goals. After earning a degree in merchandising and marketing at Ball State University, Angela moved to New York City and began her career in the fashion industry.

Working for companies like Donna Karan and Liz Claiborne, she quickly climbed the corporate ladder. After several years, a friend convinced her to accept a position as the CEO of Burberry. In 2012, she amassed Britain's highest salary, earning $26.3 million (US).

Many would consider her foolish for walking away from a job where the Queen of England bestowed the title of honorary Dame Commander of the British Empire for her contribution to British business.

But when Tim Cook of Apple Inc. proposed a career move, she felt their visions aligned and accepted the offer. Although Angela's portfolio wasn't in the tech industry, Cook pursued her because of the corporate energy she brought to the table.

One of the most exciting things about her biography is that she never pursued a job—nor did she chase money—yet incredible jobs and vast sums of money came her way. Her experience is proof positive that money is not the target—instead, it's the reward for hitting the target.

A quote from Angela inspired the theme of the 85th birthday celebration gala for Hayes Green Beach Memorial Hospital, "Energy is like emotional electricity. It gets ordinary people to do extraordinary things, which creates confidence and a safe environment where people feel like they belong and are worthy."

On more than one occasion, Angela relied on her father's wisdom, "You can teach people anything, but you cannot teach them to care."

### ENTERING THE BATTLE

Having managed teams in the corporate world and education for decades, I found that successful leaders will create an environment where members can stand out and take pride in their work.

My grandfather, a Human Resources Manager, often said, "You can only do so much. Sometimes the best decision is *not* to do something."

I find myself pulling from that concept when I feel overwhelmed or cornered by circumstances. Having experienced leadership burnout myself, I was curious about the number of leaders who had also had this experience. Did you know that sixty percent of leaders feel the burden of burnout, and twenty-six percent of them expected to leave within a year?

The statistics were a wake-up call for me. Whether we lead a business, ministry, or family, finding and embracing a work-life balance can feel like a fight. But, regardless of our leadership position, we need the courage to enter into the battle.

One of my favorite heroes of faith is David. Although most people gush over the part of the story where he brings down Goliath, I appreciate what happens right before the stone leaves the sling.

If we were to rewind things a day or two before the battle, we would cut in on the scene where King Saul offers David his armor. Cordially, David tried the gear on for size and maneuverability. Then, in a moment that mirrored a satire on Saturday Night Live, the sword outsized David's reach by a foot or more, and the armor weighed heavy on his frame. After taking a few unsteady steps, David stripped off the armor and tried to explain things to Saul.

"I appreciate your offer, but I can't use your weapons; I'm not used to them" (1 Samuel 17:38-39, NIV). The looks in the room narrowed, and soldiers shot him sideways glances. Resolute, David pushed past the crowd of critics and walked toward the battle.

As David made his way to the front lines, he could hear the Philistine's evil chants.

Even though the sun was high, David felt thick darkness. As his enemy moved forward, David bolted out of the ranks and rushed at Goliath.

Instinctively, David reached for the shepherd's pouch that hung loosely at his side. Like numerous times before, he placed a stone in the leather sling and hurled it forward. The rock landed, and Goliath slumped forward. In a free-for-all moment, David grabbed Goliath's sword and decapitated him.

I know that in our modern-day culture, that scene may seem barbaric. But ancient war stories were graphic, and death-to-the-finish moments were designed to send fear into the hearts of their adversaries.

It is worth noting that the battle could have ended differently. Who knows how things might have gone if David had let insecurity get in the way of courage? Most of us understand the pressures that come with trying to be brave when others are being critical. It's equally daunting when those in charge want us to do things their way instead of God's way. I applaud David's resolve to trust his instincts and not get caught in the backwash of another leader's ego.

## DETERMINATION IN THE FACE OF ENEMIES

Writing about gender issues, best-selling author Deborah Smith Pegues wrote, "Our best strategy is to bring our A-Game to the table along with a positive attitude and lead with care, concern, and confidence."

Being the first woman at work to take on my job description, I felt I had something to prove. In my mind, gender competition was never a part of the equation.

Unfortunately, my work culture didn't have the same outlook. Looking back, I admit to being rather naïve when I accepted the position. After all, it had taken me twenty years, often completing one course at a time to get my bachelor's degree. While in college, I worked full-time in Information Technology and shared the responsibility with my husband to raise our children and pastor a church. I made many mistakes but did my best to balance all of my responsibilities.

When I accepted the new job, I didn't doubt I would excel at my position. I was raised to embrace change and taking risks didn't scare me. One of my greatest attributes was identifying and remediating problems with a quick turnaround time.

I was shaken when I faced my first major challenge after just six weeks on the job—a complete audit of the department budget.

With only six weeks' experience, I wasn't familiar with the system or structural formatting. Committed to success, I worked late nights to identify issues, worked with the auditors, and created a plan of action that turned out great.

Over time the day-to-day operations became enjoyable. The hustle of building teams, solving problems, designing systems, and building relationships helped put me at ease. I finally fell in the *zone* and thoroughly enjoyed my job.

Then things took an unexpected turn. One day, two men walked into my office and asked if they could ask me a few questions. I smiled and welcomed them. I recognized them, but we had not been formally introduced. After a few minutes of light conversation, the meeting went in a serious direction. One of the men asked me about my previous job experience and wanted a detailed list of my qualifications.

Even though I considered it an odd question, I shared my twenty-year quest for education and my experience working in all phases of Information Technology. They continued to fire queries my way until one of them said, "We don't think you have the experience to perform this job, there has never been a woman in this role, and we don't think this will work out."

Hearing those words, my mind spun in a million different directions. For a few moments, I didn't know how to respond.

Finally, I gathered my thoughts and said, "I'm not sure where this is coming from. I have years of experience, many successful project completions, as well as relationships in the Information Technology field."

Before I could finish my thoughts, one of them interrupted me and said, "But you are a woman, and we don't think you can handle this job."

If I am honest, my emotions had me wanting to pound my desk and cry out my frustration, but knowing what was at stake, I opted for a professional response. In a commanding way, I stood up from my desk and walked to the door.

Looking at both men, I said, "I'm going to need you to leave my office and come back when you can talk to me in a professional way."

Shocked at the response, they stood and left my office. As soon as the door clicked shut, tears ran down my face. Emotionally caught off guard, I tried to gather my thoughts and decide what to do next. I considered calling my boss and human resources. My heart pounded, and I knew it was a matter of time before someone called me.

As the week dragged on, I tried to process what bothered me most. Was it because I was new to the position? Was it pride? I quickly decided that the distance of my vision and experience was equal to the title I held. I dried my tears, collected my confidence, and asked my secretary to send the person in for my next meeting.

In the end, our responses to challenging situations will make us better or leave us bitter. Although the situation was meant to shake my confidence, it made me more determined to perform at a high level. I honestly think I became a better manager because of it.

### PUSHING BACK THE FEAR

Lauren Selman is a producer, philanthropist, and award-winning director. She has worked on the production teams for the Academy Awards, the Primetime Emmys, BlizzCon, Vancouver Olympics, Golden Globe Awards, and other large live events. Speaking at an event in Santa Monica, California, she told about being *Addicted to Making a Difference.*

At age nineteen, she was asked by a friend to pedal-bike four thousand miles across the country with twenty-five other students for nine weeks to benefit Habitat for Humanity. She admitted there were things about cycling she didn't understand until she signed on for the trek, including—"you are responsible for driving, you don't know where you are, and you're vulnerable because you may not have ridden a bike in years."

Three weeks into the trip, five cyclists rode single file across Kansas. During that part of the trip, a friend lost control of her cycle and swerved in front of a car. She was propelled sixty feet into the air when the vehicle struck her and fell on the side of the road face down. Selman and another cyclist fought to revive her and administered CPR. Unfortunately, when the ambulance arrived, they gave the grim report that her friend was dead. Lauren was devastated. She realized there was nothing they could have done to save her friend's life.

Full of gut-wrenching emotions, the team had to decide whether to cancel the ride or press on and complete the journey to California. After much deliberation, they decided to press forward to the west coast.

They wanted their friend's life to matter.

As they reached the California coast forty-one days later, they stood on the Golden Gate Bridge and tied a bracelet made from their friend's shirt to the bridge. They turned to look at the country they had crossed, proud they had done it. No matter what they faced in the future, they would get back on the bike and keep on riding. Each rider raised approximately $2,500, which added over $60,000 for Habitat for Humanity.

Selman's story tugged at my heart and brought up memories of when I decided to get back on a bike and complete my journey.

Maybe, you too, have encountered situations that required doing things that bring up moments of grief or significant pain. More times than we dare admit, fear will try to keep us from moving forward.

Over the years, I have collected a number of quotes, sayings, and Scriptures that push back fear and reinforce faith. One of my favorite passages is from the ancient book of Isaiah, 41:10 (ESV) *"Fear not, for I am with you; be not dismayed, for I am your God; I will strengthen you, I will help you, I will uphold you with my righteous right hand."*

It's been my go-to Scripture when I face fear or apprehension about a situation. Because I have committed these words to memory, when I am walking through seasons that would typically bring worry, I quietly rehearse these words to my soul and am reminded of God's faithfulness.

### EQUAL CONFIDENCE

When I think about needing courage, my mind lands on Kerri Strug. Strug was a member of the *Magnificent Seven,* a group of American gymnastics competing in the 1996 Olympic games in Atlanta.

It was the first time the Russian team had participated separately from the other former countries of the Soviet Union since 1912.

On the final day of the competition, the American team trailed in second place behind Russia. Both teams focused on every aerial, lay-out, dismount, and landing. The team scores were almost even after competing on the uneven bars, balance beam, and floor exercises. The final event, the vault, would determine who carried home the gold medal. The Americans and Russians were both determined to be the best in the world.

The first four American team members completed their vaults with solid scores. Then on Dominique Moceanu's first try, she landed off-center and fell on her bottom. There was complete silence then the crowd exhaled.

On her second attempt, she fell again. As the world watched, they knew Kerri Strug's vault score would dictate whether the U.S. or Russian team would win the gold. If you weren't alive to watch this match unfold in real time, I encourage you to take a look at a highlight reel. Strug stared at the vault, took a deep breath, and sped down the runway. She landed incorrectly and also fell to the mat. When she crashed, she heard a snap. Although her ankle was aching, the adrenaline in her body helped her press forward. Having performed this vault hundreds of times, her body had memorized every motion.

Like a script from Greek mythology, Kerri Strug landed her sec-ond vault perfectly on one foot and secured the Gold Medal on her last attempt. Hopping on one foot, she received the crowd's applause as coach Béla Károlyi carried her off the mat. Pulling on her inner courage, Kerri relied on her mind and body to propel her to the top of the Olympic podium. When interviewed later, Strug said, "Pain is temporary, but pride is forever."

I was scanning through television channels when I came across a live broadcast of the 2020 Olympic Games. Pausing to watch, I no-ticed that the individual confidence level of men and women athletes were equally matched.

Thinking about *equal confidence*, I questioned why women lacked high confidence levels in the corporate world. Maybe it had to do with athletes being programmed to believe in themselves and those appointed to train them.

An article by Katty Kay, the anchor of BBC World News America, and Claire Shipman, a reporter for ABC News, explored "The Confidence Gap." The article for *The Atlantic* revealed that women are as equally competent as men, yet many women have lower self-confidence.

Although Kay and Shipman had interviewed some of the world's most influential women, they were shocked by the number of high-profile women who experienced ongoing battles with self-doubt. The article referenced a previous interview with Facebook COO Sheryl Sandberg. In her book *Lean In,* she said, "There are still days I wake up feeling like a fraud, not sure I should be where I am."

As an executive and friend of women, I assure you Sandberg is not alone in her thinking. I cannot count the number of successful women who fall for the lie that they are undeserving of the positions they worked hard to achieve.

ONE HUNDRED PERCENT SURE

Winner of two hundred NASCAR races, Richard Petty, said, "Confidence is the stuff that turns thoughts into action."

Several years ago, Hewlett-Packard tried to find innovative ways to get more women into top management positions. After reviewing personnel records, H.P. found that women applied for a promotion only when they believed they met one hundred percent of the qualifications listed on the job description.

In comparison, men at H.P. applied for a position when they thought they met sixty percent of the job requirements. In multiple studies, the data confirmed what most instinctively know about gender confidence. Although women may be overqualified and overprepared, they feel the need to hold back. "Women feel confident only when they are perfect. Or practically perfect."

I laughed when I read the results of the H.P. study, not because I found them funny, but because I had been guilty of the same thing. The study helped me change the way I conducted interviews and reviewed applications.

I found ways to factor in nonverbal cues and tried to get to know the applicant on a personal level. In a good way, I learned how to spot *confidence* and *competence*. If you have worked on a team project, you understand that sometimes a person's greatest asset is their ability to anchor people's thoughts and actions during crisis moments.

Sitting on the patio one evening, I talked with a friend about the systematic unnerving of women. Over dinner, we rambled through times we had allowed society and those close to us to snatch away our courage. We also unpacked the reasons we were so quick to let our courage go and how we could stop the cultural tide from pulling it out again.

Before we left, we decided to document every time we pushed away from an opportunity because we felt unqualified. The results of that commitment were amazing. On the first day, I made eleven entries. *Eleven times* I kept silent about an issue because I wasn't one hundred percent sure I had the perfect solution. My silence didn't stop with solutions; I also failed to correct someone three times when they incorrectly answered a question. My friend's discoveries were similar.

I was shocked and enlightened by the experience.

Emotional equity is a new buzzword in society. It is often used to describe a heart and head connection where we can step outside of ourselves and see through a new lens.

Jason Cortel, a Career Coach and Global Workforce Management Director from Phoenix, Arizona said, "Emotional equity is like banking. You either make deposits of positivity or withdrawals of negativity. The trick is to keep the emotional bank account balanced.

As a result, the occasional oops that occur are minimized and easily forgiven."

If we are not aware, our lack of confidence can be like quicksand. The more we fight the problem, the further we sink. It takes courage to widen the lens of our hearts and build lasting relationships. Maybe we should ask ourselves where and in whom we are making positive deposits. There's someone else we can't forget when making a positive deposit.

There is a courageous person within us longing to break free and conquer the world. You are strong, courageous, valuable, and a world-changer.

Get back in the battle, climb back on the bike, and stick that landing.

*Chapter Seven*

# EXPECTATIONS
# AND DREAMS

WHEN OUR CHILDREN WERE GROWING UP, MONDAY mornings were filled with chaos.

The kids ran through the house, my husband tossed dishes into the sink, and the dog chased anything that moved. Going into the week, everyone had a list of things they wanted to accomplish. Our teenagers wanted to ride to school early and hang out with friends. Gene desired coffee and to review what we needed to do that week. I wanted the kids to pack their backpacks and eat breakfast without making me late for work.

Sometimes those expectations were fulfilled; other times, we ran into brick walls.

If we are honest, the anticipation of what we would like to happen can be unrealistic. I expected that working hard would lead to instant promotion; it didn't take long to learn that dreams don't always come true in a day.

Sometimes dreams take years or, in my case, decades to come to pass. My goal of going to college, living in the dorms, making life-long friends, and graduating with a four-year nursing degree turned into a twenty-year process. Did I achieve what I set out to accomplish? Not exactly, but the journey made me strong, and I ended up in a better place. If everything had worked out my way, I would have missed out on so much more.

Conquering corporate America and higher education wasn't something I wrote in my dream journal, but it became a part of my legacy.

### WHY WE SHOULD MAKE MISTAKES

I am willing to bet that many of you started working in a restaurant or retail store. I appreciate that fact; I did too. Pictures of me wearing that ugly uniform still make me cringe. If not for the lessons learned on that job, I would toss the faded photos into the fireplace and never look back.

My dad pulled his new Ford truck into the parking lot of a shabby-looking fast-food restaurant and waited for me to get out. My hand felt glued to the handle, and I didn't budge.

Finally, he motioned me forward, but I just stared out the window. I had begged for that job but, for some reason, felt I had made a mistake.

Sensing my apprehension, Dad patted my leg and said, "It's okay, babe, just work hard, follow the instructions, and smile at the customers."

I took a deep breath, gathered my courage, and walked in, ready to work. Decades later, with many job opportunities under the bridge, I can say that advice carried me through seasons and worked in every situation.

I wish I would have clung to my father's words of wisdom more than I did. Like most stubborn teenagers, I didn't see their value until hard lessons had already been learned. I silently applaud that my parents were intuitive enough to pull back and let me make a few mistakes. I remembered a quote from Kevin Donaldson an entrepreneur and business coach, about the benefit of making mistakes, "Making mistakes is part of the process. The key to success is to make mistakes quickly, and recover quickly, and keep forging forward."

Not long after I started my first job, my mom had a stroke, then several years later, my parents divorced. The combined trauma sent me into an emotional tailspin, and my academic work suffered.

Due to my reduced grade point average, scholarship offers were retracted, and my confidence waned. I had serious doubts about whether I would achieve my academic goals, but I was determined to finish what I had started.

Tenacious and slower than expected, I completed my master's degree and then my doctorate while raising a family twenty years later.

Although the flame of my dreams flickered, it was never extinguished. Obstacles I believed would destroy me became great life lessons.

Those sticky kinds of moments made me cling to my goals when circumstances tried to snatch them away.

## SETTING EXPECTATIONS

One of my favorite quotes is from Sheryl Sandberg. "We can each define ambition and progress for ourselves. The goal is to work toward a world where expectations are not set by the stereotypes that hold us back, but by our personal passion, talents, and interests."

Setting our expectations too high can affect how we respond to the small things in life. If you have ever had your lunch order take twice as long as expected, you understand how easy it is to snap at something simple in an emotional way.

The trick to controlling our emotions is to manage our expectations. Expectation management requires that we take a step back and evaluate which situations we can handle and which remain out of our control. If you have a driven personality or are a borderline perfectionist, letting go of anything, good or bad, can be challenging.

While cheering on my granddaughter at a cross-country meet, my friend Katy shared that her daughter stayed up the night before, stressed out about winning the competition. "She's frustrated because she sets her expectations too high and can't possibly meet them. I tried to explain to her that the girl who usually wins trains hours every day for the event, but she just doesn't get it."

Her daughter ran by a few moments later with tears streaming down her face. At the end of the race, her daughter placed sixth, just seconds from winning a medal. She crossed the line, sat in the dirt, and cried.

On the drive home, I thought about Katy's daughter. Life can be challenging for teenagers, especially when so many things are pulling at them. My thoughts drifted to an article I had read about *happiness killers.*

I grabbed my phone and searched for the post when I got home. One of the things that the article mentioned was that our peace can be adversely affected when we believe that we must always do things well. I thought about how complicated it can be to live up to our expectations.

If we set the bar too high for ourselves, we will never reach the mark. If we set the bar too low, we will fail to accomplish our goals. Finding the intersection of expectations and accomplishments is the key.

It's unrealistic to think we can do everything well. Maybe you have been taught that you can achieve anything if you set your mind to a task. That's not always the case; just listen to a few rounds of karaoke.

Not everyone can sing, dunk a basketball, or earn a million dollars a year. While our spirits should remain optimistic, we have to mix in an element of realism. If we live emotionally healthy lives, we cannot keep tripping over the idea that our worth is tied to a checklist.

We are much more than the sum total of our accomplishments.

On the ride home, I used the opportunity to give my granddaughter a few words of encouragement. "You did great today, but you are more than just a number in a competition. There are dreams buried within you that you have yet to discover. It's great that you encourage Katy, but don't forget to have faith in yourself. All you can do is your best. I'm proud of you and love you, sweet girl."

Her frown changed to a smile as she began to tell me every detail about the race and what she would do differently next time.

## LIFE ISN'T ALWAYS FAIR

It's not just the expectation of managing ourselves that tears us apart. If you are like most people, you have walked through seasons where you have tried, without success, to change others. We recently saw the latest James Bond movie.

Throughout the action-packed story, Bond rescues a kidnapped scientist leading to the trail of a dangerous villain with technology capable of destroying the world. In the process, Bond faces many personal and professional challenges. He meets a woman who turns out to be the "new" 007, has many near-death experiences, and discovers he has a daughter.

As he sacrifices his life to save the world, we see his focus change to others. I thought about the identity of James Bond. Tough, decisive, sometimes lethal, yet passionate about those he loved. He didn't try to change people; he either dragged them on the journey of their lives or sacrificed his life for them. Truthfully, we recognize the only person in the world we can change is ourselves.

I cannot imagine the energy it would take to try and create an environment where everyone would satisfy our expectations.

Another common expectation is that *life is fair.* It isn't.

Expecting to bypass hardship and difficulties is like sticking our heads in the sand and denying we are at the beach. If you have been around children, you know the look that comes before the words, "It's not fair."

It's a harsh reality when things don't work out the way adults plan. It's even harder to imagine the dramatic thought that pushes through a child's mind.

Over the Christmas holiday, I tried to explain to my niece why Santa didn't bring the toy she secretly wanted. Even though I gave a long list of possible explanations, the logic was always met with, "But why?"

The more I tried to smooth things over, the more determined she became in justifying her frustration and disappointment. At one point, I wanted to say, "Nobody ever said life was going to be fair."

But I knew she would have a lifetime to figure out that cold truth.

On Instagram, I followed my friend's story of climbing Mt. Masada. The video clips and reels made the 1,500-foot rock climb look easy. Weeks later, when we caught up, she explained that the climb was filled with sand snakes, steep drop-offs, and jagged rocks. Even though she had done the climb before, it was filled with unexpected obstacles this time.

As she was reliving the journey, she said, "The climb to the pinnacle was painful, but the trip back down was a gentle slide."

Although rock climbing isn't my thing, I appreciated her resolve. Sometimes we approach situations in life with a shovel when they require an excavator. We bend and dig, and scoop and sling, only to realize that our efforts are going to take longer than we imagined. Frustration fills our hearts as we understand that good ideas often require extraordinary measures, and usually, we need help that extends beyond ourselves.

## ME-CENTRIC CULTURE

Watching an episode of *Survivor's* popular reality show reminded me how *me-centric* society has become. The game's object is to be the sole survivor, but I'm always amazed by what the participants are willing to do to earn the title.

Stranded in the islands of Fiji, eighteen "castaways" are forced to forge alliances to "Outwit, Outplay, and Outlast," all others. Throughout the entire season, they hide information, pillage the personal items of others, and straight-up lie to get information to avoid having their torches extinguished and be sent home.

Somehow, our culture has latched on to the idea that others should agree with us rather than work together to create a collective goal.

We don't always have the correct answers; we aren't always the most intelligent person in the room. I can't begin to imagine a world of *me's*, where everyone is tugging for their way. In a memorable episode of *Survivor*, a strong alliance of castaways decides to turn on a member because he has become a threat by winning physical challenges and gaining immunity.

They pretend everything is fine and blindside him in the end, choosing to protect themselves rather than being loyal to their team. We can learn a lesson from the castaways. To succeed, we need to let go of our ego and learn how to forge healthy alliances where individuality, integrity, and trust are valued.

## DOUBTING OTHERS

Research known as the "Nocebo Effect" indicates that individuals often succeed or fail based on their expectations and beliefs. It may help to clarify by mentioning a similar term, "placebo" which you are familiar with. What you may not know is that some patients who receive an inactive pill still improve. It may surprise you to know the results often depend on the patient's expectations. How often do our expectations move us forward or hold us back?

Does the effect of doubts cloud your confidence in someone? Consider that we may believe that someone is brighter because of their level of education. Or, based on someone's reputation, we may view them in high esteem even though we've never met them in person. Have you known someone that you admire based on their actions? If you are like me, you are enchanted by everyday heroes.

I ran across a blog post about Shirley White of Santa Rosa, California, an unlikely hero. She was asleep when a crash awakened her. A large fir tree had fallen from her neighbor's yard into her back yard. As she went downstairs, she glanced out the window and was horrified to see large flames leaping toward the sky.

A widow living alone, she considered calling 911, but there was no time. Instead, she grabbed a garden hose and began spraying water at the root of the flames. The wind spread the fire quickly, first to dry vines on the driveway then to the giant oak trees on the lawn. Standing close to the flames, Shirley felt the sting of the heat but refused to let the fire burn without at least trying to squelch the fire.

Luckily, a neighbor smelled the smoke and ran to help; another neighbor called 911.

The firefighters told them to move back when the trucks arrived, but Shirley didn't pay attention. She kept fighting the fire with a hose and hand rake. The next day neighbors knocked on her door and handed her a dozen roses.

They kept saying, "You're a hero. You saved the hill." Shirley didn't realize she had done anything special during the Montecito Heights fire in October 2017. Thousands of people lost everything that night in California. Shirley was a local hero because she believed that her efforts, irrespective of how small, would make a difference in a trauma-filled night.

## SHARING OUR FAILURES

My friend Carley had parents who pushed her to dream big and succeed in life. While most parents strive for their children to do well, her parents crossed the line and pressed her to the breaking point.

The pressure of having to be the first to finish the line, earn the highest academic score, marry well, and be a high-wage earner, sabotaged her potential. Carley took on too much, didn't give herself permission to say no, and quickly got overwhelmed. Her desire to win a collegiate national title in Volleyball and Track pushed her beyond her limit.

She suffered several sports injuries during that year and ended at *war* with her body. She felt like she couldn't do anything well. On a trip home from college, I gently suggested that she share her feelings with her parents.

Over dinner and some shared tears, she found a way to express her feelings without making her parents feel guilty.

Sometimes an overconfident attitude will lead us to approach difficult things in a carefree way. Have you prepared for an exam assuming that you would ace it, only to read the first question and discover you focused on the wrong material? Have you thrown yourself into a relationship only to find that the other person didn't share the depth of your feelings?

If we are not careful, life experiences can morph our expectations. As a result, we may set boundaries so tight that we don't allow ourselves to fail. Emotionally strong people understand that it is okay to make mistakes.

Mistakes are a necessary part of growth.

## BEING TOO HARD ON OURSELVES

Last week I was flipping through the sticky part of the second part of the book of Kings and stumbled upon the story of Hulda.

I retraced the historical account of her life and discovered she was a scholar from a prominent family in Jerusalem. Although she was not as widely known as other prophetic voices of her generation, she was revered for her knowledge.

Intuitively, Hulda understood that God's people had strayed far from the moral code He had given them. During the temple's renovation, when King Josiah discovered the lost book of the law, he sent messengers to Hulda. She verified the scroll's authenticity and said that disaster would strike the nation because they forgot about God.

Still, because Josiah had honored God by removing idol worship from Judah and Jerusalem, the destruction wouldn't occur during his lifetime.

The king and the people listened and adhered to her words. Her oration started a revival and solidified God's covenant with His people. Hulda believed the truth of God's word and knew that following His lead was a crucial step to a national revival. She anticipated the archaic words had the power to transform the nation, and they did.

What might happen if we were equally zealous to hear and follow the word of God? How would our lives be different? His word has the power to place our expectations in the proper order. He can balance our desires and our purposes with his. When we follow His word, striving and self-sufficiency cease.

Unfruitful desires wither and fade, and sleeping promises awake to a restored state.

It's a hard truth to own up to, but women are notoriously harder on themselves than anyone else. For whatever reason, our gender seems to find comfort in placing undue expectations on ourselves to achieve. While there is nothing wrong with doing our best, if unchecked, that mindset can land us in the ring fighting against ourselves.

In an article in *Psychology Today,* John Amodeo argued that the pursuit of perfection has an adverse effect if we expect everything to happen without the possibility of failure. Instead, we need to accept that we will make mistakes, and sometimes those mistakes lead us to golden opportunities. If we can learn to be gentle on ourselves and let loose of our ego, we may stumble into places that bring great possibilities, even enormous prosperity.

## LET THINGS HAPPEN

Have you ever seen a person who could seemingly bend reality to change your expectations? Eric Chien, a magician from Houston, Texas, pulled a fast one on the judges on an episode of *America's Got Talent*. As he introduced himself, the judges appeared unimpressed.

But as Eric masterfully created an illusion of changing cards from red to blue before their eyes and easily made coins disappear and reappear, the four judges gave him a standing ovation. Simon Cowell said it was genuinely on a different level, and Eric Chien was one of the best they had ever seen. Eric triumphed over his own delayed expectations to prove that he was one-of-a-kind to himself and the world.

If you have taken a Psychology 101 class, you may remember the self-fulfilling prophecy that "expectations become realities when you believe them."

In other words, we have the power to change our mindsets and set expectations for ourselves. It is easy to trick our minds into believing we are moving in one direction when we could be drifting in another. Managing expectations is not always easy. If we can loosen the grip of control and occasionally let things happen, we might find more joy along the journey.

I understand there are times when we need to be perfect or as close to it as possible.

If you are a surgeon about to perform brain surgery, there is no acceptable margin of error. If you are the pitcher in the final game of the World Series, falling short can cost your team a national title.

In reality, pitching a *perfect game,* a complete game without a runner reaching a base, is one of the rarest accomplishments in baseball; so rare, that it has occurred only once in a World Series Game. The pitchers set their expectations on a perfect game and let it guide their performance. Imagine you are a pitcher trying to wrap up an evenly matched game. The loud sound of the crowd fills the air, and the remaining pitch is the only thing that stands between you and a perfect game.

The odds are definitely against you. On October 8, 1956, Don Larsen of the New York Yankees threw the only perfect game in a World Series. Imagine the number of games played between 1903 and 1921, with only one *perfect game.* Imagine taking your stance, reaching back, and hurling the ball forward.

The crowd stands to their feet as the ball flies over the plate—the batter swings and misses. You pitched the perfect game. While that scenario paints a beautiful ending, what if things go in another direction? What if that last pitch connected with the bat, and the ball sailed over the outfield wall? Would you still feel that your best efforts were enough?

Although we may not be brain surgeons or major league pitchers, there's no doubt our expectations influence reality; If we don't believe we will succeed, we can be assured we won't.

CONFIDENCE IN YOUR ABILITIES

Research shows that the more we believe in ourselves, the more likely we will succeed. A Louisiana State University (LSU) study showed that people who don't believe they will succeed won't.

Believing in ourselves gives us the confidence to use more of our brains and exert more brainpower to solve problems. The study references the term *metacognition,* which is the ability to use prior knowledge to learn a task, take steps to solve it, evaluate the results, and modify our approach as needed. Although it may sound like a long and complicated definition, the philosophy is quite simple.

We are accustomed to setting expectations, developing strategies, and using our intuition. However, metacognition ensures we approach problems differently and adapt as needed.

Our mindset can move us forward or set us back. If an EMT comes upon a trauma victim, they immediately recall relevant knowledge to stabilize the patient. They *expect* to save the patient. It's essential that we believe in ourselves.

Think about the importance of expectation and confidence in becoming a teacher, social worker, CEO of a household, or entrepreneur. Do you have a strong belief in yourself? It may surprise you what we can do with a single shot of confidence mixed with a double shot of expectation.

## EXAMPLES OF SUCCESSES

Statistics show that women entrepreneurs are on the rise. Over 252 million women worldwide are entrepreneurs, and the number of female entrepreneurs has increased 114% in the last twenty years, according to Jenifer Kuadli in the legaljobs.io blog.

Young entrepreneurs often work longer hours, invest significant revenue, and spend less time with their families than they originally envisioned. Entrepreneurs may have great ideas but must execute their plans flawlessly to succeed.

Many successful women rose to the top of their field with an idea or expectation of success for themselves. For example, Angie Hicks recognized a need for qualified contractors and filled it. Founder of ANGI HomeServices, she developed a service-centric idea into a $190 million empire.

After realizing the difficulty of finding reliable contractors for home services in Columbus, Ohio, Angie partnered with William Oesterle to found Angie's List. After recruiting over one thousand members within one year, she expanded services. By 2015, the company reported over 3.2 million paid members. In July 2016, it became a *freemium* service, providing access to more than 10 million reviews. In 2021, Angie's List was rebranded to be called simply Angi. The company continues to help people find qualified contractors at the click of a button.

J. K. Rowling is the author of the *Harry Potter* book series. Surprisingly, she wrote the tetralogy as a single mom. She is also the president of Gingerbread, an organization helping single parents. Single parents can reach out to trained staff who provide practical support and networking opportunities for those who feel lonely or isolated. In addition, Gingerbread offers helpful information and resources to help single-parent families succeed.

Rowling once commented that she was prouder of her years as a single mom than at any other time in her life. At a Commencement Speech at Harvard University, she said, "We do not need magic to change the world. We carry all the power we need inside ourselves already: We have the power to imagine better."

I agree that we can all imagine better, but not all succeed because of our expectations.

Some successes are the result of tragic situations.

In 1980, a hit-and-run drunk driver killed Candy Lightner's thirteen-year-old daughter. The driver had three prior convictions and was arrested two days prior for a different hit-and-run accident. Several months later, Candy founded Mothers Against Drunk Driving (MADD) to end drunk driving and to develop legislation to help the victims of drunk drivers.

The organization has helped save hundreds, if not thousands, of lives. Both Rowling and Lightner fought tremendous battles to become successful.

In our quest for success, it is easy to make significant life commitments and then feel overwhelmed by the daily struggle of managing them. Most people fail to consider that micro-goal setting can be equally, if not more effective, than macro-goal setting.

It is possible to set realistic goals and simultaneously reach for the stars.

Brian Tracy said, "People with clear, written goals, accomplish far more in a shorter period of time than people without them could ever imagine."

I encourage you to set aside time to journal your expectations and successes every day. It's something I *try* to do every day.

When I read back through my journal, I see the many things that have been accomplished over time. I am also aware of the blessings each day that allows me to set and maintain my expectations. If you ever kept a prayer journal, I know you have experienced similar feelings when you realize how many have been answered. It's the same with our expectations and dreams.

When you feel overwhelmed or like things just haven't gone right for you, go back to your Success book, and you'll be reminded the number of successes far outnumber your failures.

# Chapter Eight

# CONSTRUCTING
# YOUR CREATIVITY

I GREATLY APPRECIATE ARTISTS WHO CAN PICK UP A BRUSH and create masterpieces that look lifelike. With tiny waves of the wrists and a few upward and downward strokes, they transform a blank canvas into a mesmerizing mosaic.

Although we are not all called to be the next Picasso or Rembrandt, God has gifted each of us with creative ingenuity. I am sure that you have naturally creative friends. Because I am wired to think analytically, I enjoy spending time with imaginative and creative people.

Their free-thinking spirits help unlock my imagination and encourage me to think and do things differently.

## MINIMIZING GIFTS

I've had friends and colleagues tell me that they weren't born with natural talents or creative abilities, and then I was stunned to hear them sing like Whitney Houston on karaoke night.

I had a friend who said she *toyed* around with pottery. She forgot to add that her pieces sold for thousands of dollars. I'm sure you have friends that undercut or minimize their gifts too.

In college, I had a professor who was an incredible pastry chef. One bite of her delicious dessert, and there was no doubt she could own a five-star restaurant. Another colleague of mine could scan through lines of computer code and instantly spot an error. Once she identified and corrected the code, she could add detailed instructions to prevent the end-user from misusing the software.

Even though her colleagues were in awe of her abilities, she failed to see the uniqueness of her talent.

Maybe God has graced you with gifts that seem ordinary to you but are impressive to others. In this age of comparison, it is easy to downplay our talent and put a lid on our potential.

## MEETING GOD ON THE BRIDGE

If you like to travel, I'm sure you have unique spots that make you pull in your breath with awe. One of my most memorable vacations was when we journeyed to Alaska with a small group of friends.

Each day, I felt like I had been dropped inside a snow globe or pushed into a postcard. The looming rock cliffs, exotic animals, and fireside talks with our friends left us wanting to stay longer. The journey was more than a vacation; it was an appointment to gather our faith around our friend Abigail.

A few weeks before we were scheduled to leave, Abigail was diagnosed with cancer. Even though we tried to convince her to reschedule the trip, she refused the suggestion.

She said, "I need this. I need to get out in nature, to relax, and hear God's voice."

Knowing about the restorative power of nature, we dropped the idea of postponing the trip and began looking forward to how God was going to use the time to minister to Abigail. Abigail needed freedom from her thoughts and to replace uncertainty with beauty.

Stepping onto the sky bridge, we took in the grand structure. On an average week, the ship hosted about 2,800 visitors, featured panoramic views, and was perfect for viewing the beautiful Alaskan landscape.

I watched as Abigail seemed to drink up the sights and sounds that enveloped her. In a way, the cancer report left us feeling more aware of how we were spending our days on earth.

The fresh awakening of our own mortality had awakened parts of our souls that had fallen into a deep sleep. As live music floated from the tiered decks, we roamed through the open spaces of the ship, and we let loose of the things that were weighing heavy in our hearts. Later that afternoon, I stood on my balcony and watched sailboats, yachts, and schooners weave through the bay.

As the sun dipped around the glass buildings and over the rim of the mountains, I felt God whisper, "It is going to be okay."

The beauty of God's creation highlighted every moment of our trip.

One of our shore excursions took us to Butchart Gardens in British Columbia. If you have never witnessed this breathtaking spot, I encourage you to place it on your travel list.

As our group walked through the winding walkways and stared at bronze sculptures, Abigail took my arm and said, "The architects must have had God's help in designing this."

She was correct; the attention to detail seemed heavenly. As we worked our way through the gardens, we took time to pray, laugh, and shed a few tears. We ended our time sharing a meal in a café with a 360-degree view of the gardens. Abigail had a positive attitude and looked for opportunities to speak life to herself and others.

I believe nature and the support of our friends helped her find healing. She would refer to those days with particular fondness throughout her treatment and recovery. Abigail's faith was powerful, and she shared it willingly. The depth of her spiritual strength was something I have always admired.

Years later, she remains cancer-free.

## CREATIVITY FOR ALL AGES

While looking out my office window, I noticed my neighbor Summer jogging behind her daughter's stroller. She had her ear pods in and seemed oblivious to her surroundings. I tried to imagine what was going on inside Summer's mind. A deep thinker and highly creative, I felt sure she was listening to a motivational podcast.

For a moment, I was slightly envious of her youth. But then I quickly remembered that the under thirty club isn't the only one that God pours creativity into. Some of the world's most innovative ideas are inspired by those who have lived fifty or more years and cross-collaborate with younger generations.

## FINDING BEAUTY IN IMPERFECTIONS

When I first met Diana, I was immediately drawn to her and knew we would be lifelong friends.

Diana designs jewelry and has a way of taking basic elements and shaping them into exquisite pieces. She discovered her gift for designing jewelry after coming across a stone in a mine in Montana.

While exploring a cave, her flashlight fell on a rough, dark-colored stone along the wall's edge. While most of us would have passed it up as useless, Diana saw its potential.

Although the stone would have been nothing more than just a rock to many of us, Diana saw it as a beautiful gem, left in its original form. Running my fingers around the jagged parts of the stone, I asked why she didn't smooth the sides and polish the stone.

She explained that leaving it in its natural state reminded her that peace and tranquility can be found in dark, unpredictable places. She clung to that idea, created beautiful art pieces, and gave them to women walking through a difficult season—a reminder to them, that there was beauty in their imperfections.

Diana ministers to women regularly and is a fantastic mentor and artist. Her ministry positively affects the lives of hundreds of women.

## CONNECTING WITH THE CREATOR

In the book *Soul Keeping: Caring for the Most Important Part of You,* best-selling author John Ortberg said, "The self is not the soul. The self is a stand-alone, do-it-yourself unit, while the soul reminds us we are not made for ourselves or by ourselves. The soul always exists before God. Your soul connects your thoughts, your sensations, your emotions, your will, and integrates them into an entire being."

After reading those words, I thought about how solitude, or alone time, allows us to disconnect from our long lists of responsibilities and over-stuffed lives.

Carving out time for prayer will enable us to talk with God and then listen for his response. I'm sure that most of us long for extra hours in the day to relax, meditate, and connect with our Creator.

It can be challenging to work self-time into our schedules.

Sometimes we have to fight to lay aside things that pull at our attention or press past situations that demand our emotional and mental energy to take care of ourselves and experience spiritual freedom.

Life can feel like a fight for freedom more than we may admit. Anxiety can sabotage our moods, stresses can unnerve our emotions, and fear can leave us feeling like failures. But it is in those seasons we must rise up and contend for our peace.

Elanor Roosevelt said, "It isn't enough to talk about peace. One must believe in it. And it isn't enough to believe in it. One must work at it."

Our different needs and lifestyles require us to use creativity, forethought, and prayer to succeed. We must recognize that maintaining our soul is just as important as keeping our physical health. Sometimes we need solitude, silence, and a safe place to grow.

Spiritual change is like a pendulum swinging back and forth, from peaks of success to valleys of challenges and back up again. Whatever brings forth continuous movement and change will lead us to a connection with God.

When we move toward being more like Christ, we think outside the box and open up the brain's creativity to a floodgate of ideas and perspectives.

The book of Genesis gives a detailed account of how God created us in his image. Subconsciously, I pull in a breath when I imagine God pouring his breath into the first man and woman.

What a fantastic moment it must have been for creation to witness the formation of the first humans. During the rough times, I think we forget that we are made in God's likeness, meaning we have access to his wisdom, knowledge, and creativity. Every day we have the opportunity to discover unique aspects of our creative genius.

As I sit and watch the sunset, I notice the variety of colors on the trees displaying a perfect cohesive color pallet. Even something as simple as a sunset is purposeful, artful, and designed to unlock our imagination.

God longs to lead us into new realms of creativity, unlock innovative ideas, inspire creative thoughts, and help us visualize the future. The same creative power that formed the world will help us reimagine ours.

## DIFFERENT TYPES OF CREATIVITY

While working through some research, I stumbled upon some truths that helped me better understand the link between science and creativity. Deliberate creativity is purposeful and combines skill and capabilities while spontaneous creativity requires knowledge and inspiration. I found that *deliberate and cognitive* creativity is developed through research, trial, and error.

It is the type of creativity that Thomas Edison used to create the light bulb. While *spontaneous and cognitive* creativity is what prompted Isaac Newton's discovery of gravity. Once Newton's mind was open to various ideas and thoughts, the simple act of an apple falling from a tree gave birth to the law of gravity.

*Deliberate and emotional* creativity exists when we produce positive thoughts, even when stressed. It begins with emotions and feelings and requires reflection and quiet time. Most of us are familiar with *spontaneous and emotional* creativity. Talented artists and musicians must have the inspiration and skill to create masterpieces. *Aesthetic creativity* represents artists, writers, and musicians who show their personality, emotion, point of view, or perspective. Whether we are paint slingers, rap artists, jewelry artisans, or weekend karaoke warriors, we have to work at sharpening our skills and giving room for our imagination to inspire others.

If you feel like you are more administrative or analytical and lack creative talent, I encourage you to do things that will pull out your creativity.

Invest time reading a novel, pursuing an advanced degree, watching a TED Talk, or visiting a museum. Those with kinetic imagination can work with paint, and photography, visit galleries or read magazines and blogs related to our field. People with emotional or interpersonal creativity can meet new people or study leadership and human dynamics.

Of course, it is always valuable to hear inspirational speakers or go to a movie premiere. If you want to learn more about unlocking your creative side, I encourage you to take an online quiz that will help you identify your creative traits. You can access the quiz at: https://www.mindtools.com/pages/article/creativity-quiz.htm.

You may be surprised by what you discover.

## CREATIVE CULTURES

Early in my career, I learned the importance of finding talented people and then creating a culture that would amplify their success. I discovered how to build teams that would carry the vision, execute strategy and gain high results.

I spent hundreds of hours learning team-building theory, but the most practical application came from visiting Apple headquarters in Cupertino, California. A team of educators from Texas was invited to provide input related to technology in education. The buildings were arranged in a perfect campus-style atmosphere conducive to learning.

Daily, friendly Apple employees guided us to the building, where we met in their conference rooms. Motivational quotes were placed throughout the building, and everything from the lighting to the large conference table and comfortable chairs were purposefully in place. Our Apple team leader took charge and discovered our areas of expertise.

Watching him lead the team and establish sub-teams enlightened us as we worked through the agenda. Free time allowed us to participate in creative activities and access the latest technology.

Watching global company leaders in their element provided the perfect collaborative learning experience. It was a great example of nontraditional creativity. I will never forget the experience knowledge and the practical application of theory demonstrated that week.

It reshaped my view of the creation process and pushed me to explore the boundaries of my creativity.

## CREATIVITY DEFINED AND COMMUNICATED

Although there are hundreds of definitions for the word *creativity,* Andy Eklund, a trainer for businesses, communications, and creativity, describes creative learning into two categories.

*Creative Problem Solving* focuses on understanding the actual problem and generating ideas to solve it. Eklund believed it didn't have to be a big idea but needed to differentiate brands, attract customers' attention, and reinforce purchasing decisions or habits. Eklund described creativity as "The act of combining previously unconnected ideas, concepts, information, or elements to make something new, unique, or useful."

I'm sure you are familiar with big ideas. There are ways to communicate information about a product or concept to customers by creating solid messages. One of the most successful advertising campaigns of the 1990s was Nike's "Just Do It" slogan.

That brand component allowed the company to increase sales from eighteen percent to forty-three percent in the North American domestic sports shoe market. In just ten years, the company reportedly leaped from $877 million to $9.2 billion in worldwide sales.

"Just Do It," and the swoosh remain trademarks associated with Nike today. Nike's big idea transformed the company brand into a household name.

## THE CREATIVITY PROCESS

David Ogilvy, a British advertising tycoon, known as the "Father of Advertising," said, "Big ideas come from the unconscious. This is true in art, science, and advertising. But your unconscious has to be well informed, or your idea will be irrelevant. A key to creative thinking is to stuff your conscious mind with information, then unhook your rational thought process."

Have you ever wondered what happens during the creative process?

The first step is *incubation,* which capitalizes on teamwork, empowerment, and building trust. Developing a vision statement or a lesson plan are excellent examples.

The next step is *imagination* which encourages experimentation, exploration, and unique visions, followed by *improvement* which focuses on incremental improvements, systematic approaches, and clarifying problems. Think of this step as developing a vaccine for a pandemic. Imagine the exact steps to be followed and the amount of problem-solving required.

The last step is *investment* which fosters rapid goal achievement, competitive strategies, and problem resolution. When I think of the last piece of the creative process I think of Coca-Cola and the successful creation of a variety of flavored drinks we love.

The cycle can be effective when we unleash our unique, creative abilities. Greater understanding of the creative process can help us know our Creator better.

## GOD CREATED

When God created the universe, He creatively commanded the energy of the elements.

The opening words of the book of Genesis described it this way: *"In the beginning, God (prepared, formed, fashioned, and) created the heavens and the earth"* (Genesis 1:1, AMPC).

The entire book contains a detailed account of how God created the elements and brought to life all living things.

As I meditated on those passages, I realized how much creativity God gave to His creation. In Jason Goldman's article, "Creativity: The Weird and Wonderful Art of Animals," he explained what most of us overlook: animals create art and derive joy from them.

Goldman referenced the Vogelkop gardener bowerbird with drab, olive-brown feathers that make it hard to spot against the dirt it lives on. The male birds build elaborate and decorated structures called bowers. In some places, the tall towers are made of sticks resting upon a round mat of dead moss, decorated with snail shells, acorns, and stones.

They create woven towers built upon a platform of green moss adorned with fruits, flowers, and butterfly wings in other places. The male bowerbirds are considered creative engineers, placing each piece with exact precision—UCLA physiologist Jared Diamond was one of the first researchers to study the birds' elaborate bowers.

He discovered that bower building was not entirely instinctive. He found the creative process was based on culture, and decisions were made with care. "In other words, the Bowerbirds are animal artists—at least in the sense that they create unique things humans and birds find esthetically pleasing."

Even if you are not an outdoor enthusiast, you may be surprised by the mental abilities of mammals and sea creatures.

If you have ever taken a dolphin cruise, you know that their interaction with humans is soul-stirring. Considered the second most intelligent animal on earth, dolphins have a sizeable brain-to-body ratio, show great emotion, and mimic humans.

New findings suggest they may be the second-sneakiest mammals on earth. At the Institute for Marine Mammal Studies in Mississippi, dolphins were shown how to pick up litter in their tanks in exchange for fish. A dolphin named Kelly discovered that if she hid scraps of trash under a rock in her tank, she could tear the paper into multiple pieces and get more fish.

Researchers applauded her creative ingenuity, and so do I.


CREATIVITY REMINDERS

Remind yourself what seems ordinary to you is a tremendous contribution to others. Whether your creativity is expressed in traditional or non-traditional forms, it's your gift.

Take time to think about something you created that you were proud of. It could have been as simple as helping your child with a school project or preparing a table arrangement for a meal with friends. How can you recreate an atmosphere to use your creative abilities regularly? Is there something you can change that enables you to think more clearly and let natural creativity flow? Think about the past week. How did you spend your time? Were you overextended? Is it possible to detangle some of your responsibilities and allow yourself the freedom to do something you enjoy? Can you identify the most significant "time wasters" in your life? I have a friend Margo who has difficulty saying no. She is the first to take on a new responsibility at work and volunteers at her kids' school. In addition, she takes part in community outreach activities. However, she relaxes and rejuvenates her mind when you get her away from her responsibilities. I've never known anyone better at compartmentalizing their life.

Rest is essential, and it's entirely in our span of control. Next week, concentrate on things that allow you to take advantage of creative moments. Read a book, sleep, take a long walk with a friend, curl up on the couch, watch a movie, or binge-watch a series.

View this as a positive exercise with no competition and no one to check your progress at the end of the week. Give yourself the gift of time to spark the imagination you had as a child when you used crayons to create portraits.

Remember a time before you were taught life was serious. Being creative isn't about solving life's issues; it's about constructing an environment where you can allow yourself to thrive.

## Chapter Nine

# INTIMIDATION - THE SUBCONSCIOUS FEAR

A s much as I love plunging into the ocean, I have learned that sea creatures are not fond of humans poking around in their space.

Divers know beautiful starfish can become aggressive if agitated. Uniquely designed with regenerative qualities, starfish will sacrifice limbs if it means escaping an attack. Refusing to be intimidated, they intuitively grasp the idea that it is better to come away from a fight scarred up than to die a needless death.

I wish I could say that most people have as much grit as a starfish, but my conscience won't let me. Situational paralysis has a way of making us pull our emotions inward. If we are not careful, we will hide in our shells.

### FAITH FLATTENERS

Our grandkids used our air mattress as a makeshift bed in the game room the other day. Excitement turned to disappointment when the PVC material went flat like our morning pancakes. After half an hour, I eventually found a tiny hole in the corner of the mattress.

Even though we tried to patch the leak, the air kept finding a way out. Staring at the plastic, I thought about how something so small could destroy a product designed to hold hundreds of pounds of weight.

Then, I thought about how small confidence leaks can flatten our faith.

I know we don't have time, but what if we added up all the instances when we let negative words or actions deflate our expectations?

Would we regret not fulfilling a dream because someone threw daggers at our character? Would we be annoyed because we allowed the opinions of others to overpower our enthusiasm?

It would be sad to realize that our dreams could be deflated with a verbal prick or two, but I have seen that scenario play out. I am sure you have too. I have watched jealous coworkers flatten the ambition of their colleagues, and one spouse snatch away the security and support from the other.

For whatever reason, the downside of human nature seems to think that there is strength in making others weak.

Decades ago, my husband and I pastored a church. Young and naïve, I didn't understand how my talents could help our congregation. I didn't have the confidence to stand before people and preach, and I had no musical talent.

Something as simple as calling on me to do karaoke would have seemed like a death sentence. For years, a spirit of intimidation held my gifts hostage to my fears.

Even though I had confidence in other areas of life, I felt paralyzed to stand before people and share my soul.

Years would pass before I realized I was a prisoner of my emotions.

Past hurts replaced self-confidence with insecurities. I believed the lie that my words didn't carry weight or that I wasn't worthy of being heard. Like a steel trap, negative thoughts snapped at my courage and captured my ability to communicate.

One of my greatest regrets is the years I spent hiding behind silence.

I didn't find my courage overnight, but a turning point happened when I listened to a message on forgiveness. The truth is I had not fully forgiven a family member. I had allowed bitterness to dim parts of me that once burned bright.

As I heard the message on forgiveness, I let the Holy Spirit shine his light on the dark areas of my heart. When I saw how deep the darkness had become, I closed my eyes and released the blackened parts of my soul to God. It took a while to rebuild the broken parts of my heart. But when the pieces came together, my confidence was restored.

## INTIMIDATION AND INDECISION

Tucked away in my journal are the words, "There is a stubbornness about me that can never bear to be frightened at the will of others. My courage always rises at every attempt to intimidate me."

This quote from one of my favorite pieces of classic literature, *Pride and Prejudice,* caught my attention earlier in life and made its way to the pages of my journal as something to guard against.

When I find my confidence challenged by others, the spicy and outspoken part of me rises to voice my opinion, often disguising a defense mechanism.

As you may understand, intimidation evokes deep-seated feelings of inadequacy, triggering a fight-or-flight response.

If I don't pause for a minute, my mind can take me to a place where an emotional response could disengage me from level-headed thinking. Whether you stand up to the intimidation or back away from it, there is action required on your part. Can you recall a time when you were intimidated and were surprised by the feelings that took over your thought and emotional processes?

While building our new house, I considered the impact of the journey we were about to take. I mean, I'm an educated professional woman.

How hard could it be? Trust me when I say I had no idea—being responsible for every minute detail from brick and shingles to light fixtures and everything in between would be so overwhelming.

One sunny summer day, my husband and I visited the plumbing store to pick out fixtures. I was intimidated from the moment I walked in.

Who knew there would be a wall of everything from sink fixtures to showerheads and tub fillers? Everything I had taken for granted now mattered.

The salesperson began to show us the layout. "Here are the sink fixtures, 'Chrome, Matte Black, Bronze, Gold, Brushed Nickel …' You'll find them organized by style and finish."

I froze and stood staring at the wall of fixtures. Why was I immediately intimidated by a sink fixture, of all things?

My husband, unaccustomed to my indecision, walked over to one of the fixtures, pointed, and said, "I like this one."

I diverted my attention to the fixture, and it was identical to the one we had in our bathroom.

He said, "Come on, you have managed million-dollar budgets and large projects, and you can't pick a faucet? Just get what you like." I shook my head in disbelief that I had allowed something so simple to set me off balance. It wasn't because I couldn't decide; I was afraid to choose. Isn't it ridiculous that something so simple can take us out of our game?

It doesn't take much for people or situations to snatch away our confidence. If you've endured the pain of public speaking, you know what emotional stabs in the stomach feel like. Walking onto a platform can feel like walking a gangplank.

At that moment, all the hours of preparation can seem inadequate. One look at the crowd can release a deluge of doubts, and we can lose sight of what we are doing. Whether we are called to speak to thousands or the neighbor across the street, we can find confidence in knowing that God will fill our mouths with hope and truth.

Can we come to terms with what intimidates us? For example, would you be intimidated by talking to a judge in court even though you did nothing wrong? Would a bully intimidate you? How about a formidable opponent in a game or an argumentative coworker?

Recognizing intimidation may have nothing to do with us and everything to do with our perception of others is an important discovery.

## PUSHING AWAY OUR FEARS

Some of the world's most progressive leaders have had to learn how to fight off internal fears.

If you are familiar with the Apostle Paul, you realize his legacy would have been incomplete without Timothy.

History reveals that Timothy's mother was Jewish, and his father was Greek. His familiarity with both cultures made him a prospective protégé of Paul's. Recognizing Timothy's potential, Paul installed him as a pastor in the city of Ephesus.

Immediately, Timothy faced crucial hardships in leading the church and congregants forward. Recognizing challenges could undermine Timothy's authority, Paul addressed any insecurities by reminding him that God is the source of confidence.

In an intimate letter to Timothy, Paul reminds him that *"For God gave us a spirit not of fear but of power and love and self-control"* (2 Timothy 1:7, ESV). Taking those words to heart, Timothy found the courage to lead without looking over his shoulder.

One of my favorite scriptures poses a rhetorical question.

It simply asks, *"If God is for us, who can be against us?"* (Romans 8:31b, ESV).

Read that through again. One more time.

That one question should push all of our fears off the cliff. When intimidation creeps in, don't bury yourself beneath the blanket of self-doubt. Instead, think of the times you have been successful. Bring to mind winning moments that boost your faith and remind you to take authority over negative situations.

Instead of isolating yourself from the world, turn to God's word for direction, strength, and faith.

### OVERCOMING ANXIETY WITH OTHERS

Our experiences play a role in responding and engaging with the world.

If you had a stern upbringing, you know what it is like to be pinched for whispering too loud in public. From an early age, most of us were taught that our words, and sometimes the volume of our words, reflect our character.

But in our defense, sometimes reactions are simply involuntary. If you have ever crossed paths with a celebrity, you understand what it is like to forget your first name, maybe even how to talk at all.

Sometimes intimidation pulls out unexpected reactions.

My friend Bailey was an outgoing person who had an opinion about everything until it came time to talk to strangers.

It was interesting to watch the girl who was the life of the party suddenly go silent when someone new walked in. At first, I didn't understand her reaction and thought she was snobbish.

But, one night at a football game, I realized that her reactions were genuine. Inwardly, she fought wars that only her closest friends could have recognized. At half time, when our group made our way to the concession stand, Bailey smiled and was friendly to the people in our section, but when we reached the end of the bleachers where my neighbor, Aaron, was sitting, she froze.

Her posture changed, and her eyes fell to the ground. She raced for the steps and disappeared out of sight without looking up.

When I passed Aaron, he rolled his eyes and asked, "What's up with your friend?" Then, he laughed and said, "Tell her not to worry; I don't bite."

When I caught up with Bailey, she looked horrified. Fighting back the tears, she rambled, "Why do I do that? I'm so uncomfortable around people I don't know. I don't know what to say. How can I change?"

I said, "You can start by smiling and saying 'Hi.'"

I encouraged her to take things slow and learn how to engage on a small scale instead of jumping into a relationship at full throttle. Over time, Bailey learned how to overcome her anxiety and mastered the art of introduction.

In a full-circle twist, she became a successful real estate attorney and interacts with people worldwide. It took work to step out of her comfort zone and step into the freedom of accomplishing her dreams.

WORKING WITH LEADERS

I am sure many of us have been intimidated by the opinions or reactions of a boss, pastor, or leader. In western culture, it is not uncommon for leaders to use intimidation as a management method.

Working for an authoritarian leader is not easy, especially if you are used to a democratic working environment. Even strong team members grow weary of bosses who are manipulative or aggressive.

Having worked with solid and driven leaders, I have watched those in authority cross the line of what is considered mentally healthy or emotionally constructive.

I wish I could erase the memory of publicly humiliated colleagues without just cause, but I can't. In fact, I think of them often and am amazed that they survived the drama that was allowed to dominate the corporate world. At this stage in life, I admire leaders who are confident enough to care for those they're assigned to lead. Just as my friend was intimidated by others, it can be intimidating to work with overbearing bosses.

## IGNORING THE INTIMIDATORS

From a young age, my sisters and I were taught to be strong, have an opinion, and not be afraid to share it.

That ideology took root, and we are still the first to stand up for our beliefs. There were five girls in my family, and if you have a teen-age girl or a family member with a teenage girl, you understand the challenge of allowing strength without stubbornness.

Without loads of self-confidence and the ability to face intimidation head-on, my poor parents would have never survived our adolescent years. They understood their leadership roles at work, home, and church. Of course, we challenged their authority, tried their patience, and provided them with many opportunities to speak correction, strength, and truth.

If we don't understand our roles as leaders, we cannot help others find their center and reach their goals.

My family spends a significant amount of time watching sports.

As a former athlete, Gene appreciates the players' mental toughness and physical stamina. I enjoy the gritty part of the game, the "trash-talking," extra pushing, and stare-downs. The thought of someone using verbal bait or eye contact to psychologically mess with a competitor makes me laugh.

Sometimes those ploys work, but athletes are trained to push through pain, verbal jabs, and less-than-perfect conditions. Truthfully, it doesn't matter whether we are staring across the gridiron or across the board room; intimidation can affect our confidence and take our heads out of the game.

The goal of oppression is to distract us from our focus.

In the Olympic Games in Rio, before the semi-final heat of the 200 butterfly race, defending Olympic champion Chad Le Clos tried to intimidate top medalist Michael Phelps. As they prepared for the semi-final showdown, Le Clos shadowboxed in front of Phelps.

Ignoring the gesture, Phelps stared forward and listened to his headphones. Although he noticed Le Clos's tactic, he used intimidation to improve his performance.

Phelps said, "There wasn't a shot I was losing that race, and if I did, I was leaving everything in the pool."

Phelps won and beat Le Clos by over a second. Phelps went on to win the final race by four-hundredths of a second and was the gold medal recipient.

## ROOTS OF INTIMIDATION

The root of intimidation is fear. Wouldn't it be great if we could take charge of our emotions without buying into the lie that we are somehow less significant than others?

When we fall into the comparison trap, we create unhealthy contrasts that produce low self-esteem and anxiety. Intuitively, we will withdraw from situations that stack our gifts or talents against others. Withdrawing from others without explanation creates more social tension and adds to our insecurities. The psychological cycle can be explained:

Stage 1: Insecurity
Stage 2: Reasoning
Stage 3: Withdrawal
Stage 4: Misunderstanding
Stage 5: Added Insecurity

If we are to stop the cycle of intimidation, we must acknowledge and deal with our insecurities.

One way to overcome intimidation is to stop avoiding situations where you feel intimidated.

Instead, face your fears, push back unhealthy feelings, and become more assertive. Don't allow others to control your emotions. When you give your emotional power to others, you surrender the ability to navigate the outcome of a situation.

Second, learn to expect positive things to happen. Imagine the situation turning out in your favor. Visualize the best result possible and live out of that image.

My grandmother reminded me that we base ninety percent of our decisions on situations that will never happen.

As I got older, she further instilled that idea by challenging me to write down everything I worried about for a week. I accepted her challenge, and at the end of the week, I handed her my list, and we went over the things I had scribbled down.

There were about a hundred items on the list, and as she predicted, only two of them happened. What I perceived as a cheeky challenge became a valuable life lesson. It's not that I don't occasionally struggle to overcome worry because there are times that I do. But now, I view fears in a healthier way. I take time to meditate and offer those concerns to God in prayer.

## RECOVERY FROM INTIMIDATION

In today's business environment, intimidation is an age-old tactic used to leverage one's competitors.

In a negotiation session I was in years ago, an administrator took control of the meeting and ranted about restrictions, programs, and communication.

It was clear from the moment he pushed into the board room that he was there to let off steam and not make clear-minded decisions. Jon, the team leader and a great communicator, allowed him to ramble for about five minutes, then raised his head and said, "That's enough. You've had the opportunity to speak and have managed to insult everyone at the table. I heard your concerns, and you and I will discuss them later."

Silence fell over the room, and the administrator left the meeting. The team let out a collective sigh of relief when the door clicked shut. Jon changed the tone of the conversation and asked his assistant to bring in fresh coffee. When the meeting started back up, we worked through the schedule as if nothing had happened.

That is what highly effective teams do; they recover.

We went through the business plan and discussed each item, allowing team members to contribute to the conversation. We chose to shake off the negativity and move forward.

Did I feel intimidated by the administrator's aggression? Yes, because some of his comments were directed at me. Thankfully, I held on to my peace and refused to react.

I've learned that intentional actions prevail over emotional reactions. Later that day, I received a call from my boss.

He said, "Well, that was intense. Are you okay?"

I said, "Of course, I knew he was upset with the situation and not with me. I'm used to being the lone girl at knights of the round table." The comment made us laugh, and we moved on to discuss future ideas.

It can be challenging to provide people with impromptu information in the tech industry. When customers reach an information specialist, they are usually mentally frazzled and emotionally overwhelmed. I've been on both sides of this scenario and empathize with those who need information and those working to provide it. Several years ago we were all challenged to take a running leap outside the box and become information trustees and technology scholars. Not only were we dealing with a pandemic but were flung into new mini societies with a plethora of complex challenges.

In 2020, state agencies instructed schools to provide online curriculums to students.

Unfortunately, those in charge did not consider the number of students who did not have access to the internet or were not trained to submit assignments virtually. To complicate matters, teachers were instructed to work around the clock to compile their lessons and post online resources.

Imagine the challenges schools faced in providing online resources for each student. Consider the added confusion of parents trying to navigate the challenges of working from home and helping children with schoolwork with limited resources. Those working in the IT (information technology) industry were overwhelmed with demanding calls and angry customers.

Everyone felt mentally taxed and emotionally drained. I can't tell you how many hours I spent on the phone with parents who were upset with technological glitches and had exhausted the hope of finding solutions to the problems. For the first time, I realized a large number of people are intimidated by change and innovation.

Facing major deadlines, our team discovered innovative ways to synchronize our efforts.

For those who did not have access to the internet, we developed a way to provide them with internet service without leaving the safety of their cars. Teams mounted Wi-Fi public access points in parking lots adjacent to schools and other public locations. Our primary concern was for various agencies to come together for the common good.

Together we took a challenging time in history and made innovative things happen.

Leonard Ravenhill said, "A man who is intimate with God is not intimidated by man."

While writing this chapter, I realized that at the root of intimidation is the subconscious fear that we are inadequate, less than enough, or in some way significantly flawed.

Reading through the Bible, I noticed that God did everything in an "all-in way." He never retracted a decision or second-guessed his plan.

Maybe we should model that example. Imagine how differently this year might be if we faced situations with complete resolve and determination. It is time we shut the door on superficial opinions and put negative comments in their rightful place.

Once we take ownership of the power that God has given to us, we can move forward into our futures without fear of failure. It is time we activate our faith and take steps in the direction of our destiny. If we pick up anything this year, it should be the determination to defeat the spirit of intimidation.

As believers in Christ, we are called to be brave and courageous, not beaten down by intimidation.

Throughout history, men and women of faith were called upon to change culture during challenging times. Some faced the darkness of civil persecution, such as the gallows and crucifixion; others endured social injustice and religious persecution.

But each person faced their fears head-on and relied on their faith to propel them forward.

I am sure you have a list of powerful women you admire because they stepped over the opportunity to be pushed aside and stood tall in the face of challenging circumstances.

I hope that we can model their strength as we go throughout this year. May we embody the courage of women who used their opinions to turn the tide of culture, mothers who shaped dynasties, female warriors who commanded armies, and fearless women who refused to be ignored by historians.

Yes, I know how daunting the task is to fill shoes that we think are too big for us. We should take comfort in knowing that if they don't fit us now, or feel comfortable at first, eventually, our feet will fill out the shape, and we will feel comfortable leaving our footprints in history.

*Chapter Ten*

# NURTURING UNCONVENTIONAL ORIGINALITY

MANDY SAT ON THE PORCH HUMMING NOTES AS HER hands gently moved across the guitar strings.

The lyrics flowed out of her soul and spilled onto the paper. Over the last few weeks, Mandy had felt a freshness in her acoustic creations. Her songs, like her personality, were original and deeply soulful. She turned down recording contracts as a young artist because music labels wanted her to produce content that conflicted with her morals.

So instead of selling out, she paired her songs with a lesser-known independent label. Fans appreciated her authenticity and championed her work.

As a child, Mandy was high-spirited and fearless. Her brave, if not reckless, actions kept her parents eyeing her every move. If left alone too long, Mandy would dive into the deep end of the pool, wander down the neighborhood streets, or slip off into the woods. It wasn't that she was rebellious, she was just curious. Her independent way of exploring the world often rubbed those in authority the wrong way. Most teachers thought Mandy was lazy or absent-minded. When other children comprehended and completed assignments with ease, she drew pictures of ponies. A beautiful contradiction of all things average, she struggled with tasks like counting money but had the artistic ability of Monet.

For years, Mandy struggled and sometimes failed to fit in with the world around her. Things slowly improved when a fourth-grade teacher discovered Mandy had a learning disability and helped her champion her challenges. The teacher encouraged Mandy's parents to enroll her in lyrical dance, choir, and art classes to help funnel her creativity in positive ways. The suggestions sparked a part of Mandy's soul that had fallen asleep, and she responded like daffodils in early spring.

### THE IMPORTANCE OF THE JOURNAL

H.S. Crow said, "Creative people have it hard. There is always something trapped in their noggins yearning to escape like a caged animal, both too free and wild to contain."

A few years ago, I stumbled on a stack of high school and college journals. As I scanned through the pages, I couldn't help but notice my naivety.

Looking at the loopy hand-drawn hearts and flowers scrawled along the edges, I wondered why the colorful drawings didn't seem to go along with the downcast words. Maybe there was a part of my heart that longed to be free but felt chained to some kind of pain.

As I pushed the journals to the back of the closet, I wondered when that creative girl first lost her confidence. Was it the time when someone said her art didn't look true to life, when the professor said she had no shot at the scholarship, or when male colleagues said she didn't belong in their profession? I also wondered if the more mature version of her still tries to camouflage the pain when she writes in her journal.

In what areas have you tried to flower-up failures, cover over conflict, or draw around disappointments?

Whether we keep journals, file away our thought, or voice record our memories, consider that more than our words are captured in those archives.

On Sundays, my friend Lisa creates a written record of her week to measure her moods. My friend Noel uses her journal to track essential decisions. She says that simple act helps her remember why she made specific choices.

A study in *Scientific American* found value in journaling for older adults. In the survey, 76 percent who spent twenty minutes writing about their thoughts and feelings for three consecutive days before a medical biopsy were fully healed eleven days after the procedure.

Other sources suggest that even one hour of writing about disturbing events helps participants make sense of situations and reduces stress. The simple act of journaling can produce long-term improvements in mood, decrease stress levels, and increase the chances of fighting diseases like cancer.

Although others may consider journaling nothing more than entries in a diary, journals can be essential tools for exploring our thoughts and unlocking our originality. While journaling may not be for everyone, media can provide us with an outlet to express our original ideas in ways we never dreamed possible.

## CHARACTERISTICS OF CREATIVES

Every year in Austin, Texas, thousands of *digital creatives* worldwide gather to discuss innovative ideas and network with other professionals.

The South by Southwest (SXSW) event began in 1987. It provided collaborative learning tracks focused on film, music, culture, and technology. The emphasis on interactive media remains a drawing point for creative minds and those exploring the tech industry.

In 2017, Adam Grant, a top-rated professor at the Wharton School of Business and one of the world's top 40 most influential management thinkers under 40, delivered a compelling interactive keynote address, *Inspiring a Culture of Originality.*

According to Grant, original people share common characteristics. They are *Risk-averse and don't want to fail.* Overall, original people can get past *idea generation* and move to *idea selection.* Let's take a closer look at this.

You can agree that we all have ideas. Some are good, some not so good. The reality is we can conceptualize these ideas, so there isn't a lack of creativity; there's a fear of failure. So we evaluate ideas until we find one that's worth it and make a selection.

Do you remember ideas you had in the past, but your fear of failure stopped you from pitching them? What about concepts you had complete confidence in and couldn't wait to share? Is it possible for you to identify a pattern in both your good and bad ideas and trace it back to how you felt at the time?

Grant said, "Imperfections are the flavor in an otherwise bland world," during his presentation.

I typed those words at the top of my file to meditate on them throughout the day. I considered what a *bland world* might look like. Having lived in Louisiana, where spicy food and jazz bands are a way of life, it was hard to imagine any aspect of life as *bland.*

In my culture, flavorless food was considered a failure.

During his speech, Grant challenged the audience to examine themselves and their thoughts about originality. The activity included making a list of their favorite ideas for creating anything, a cake, a painting, a house design. After completing their lists, audiences were instructed to rank their ideas from favorite to least favorite.

He pointed out that typically one's second idea is the best. The first ideas are those in which we are highly invested and unable to see potential flaws or pitfalls.

Grant shared that in 2003 when he prepared to move across the country, he started his own social media platform to meet students who planned to attend Harvard. It grew to over two hundred users, and many of them discovered new friends, romantic relationships, and roommates in the online community.

But, according to Grant, he did not have the technical skills or creativity he needed to advance the platform. As a result, he didn't realize the potential until Mark Zuckerberg came up with Facebook. Grant didn't focus on what he didn't do but used his energy to obtain a teaching position at a prestigious university where he could affect the lives of others. The position enabled him to influence today's business leaders. Grant works with business leaders who create organizational climates where people are empowered to move their creative ideas forward in a secure way.

## PRODUCTIVITY AND CREATIVE BLOCKS

Those who don't follow the traditional path to success are often characterized as different, yet they lead some of the most profitable companies in the world. For example, Steve Jobs, former CEO of Apple, Inc., said,

"Here's to the crazy ones, the misfits, the rebels, the troublemakers, the round pegs in the square holes … the ones who see things differently–they're not fond of rules, and they have no respect for the status quo … They push the human race forward, and while some may see them as the crazy ones, we see genius because the people who are crazy enough to think that they can change the world are the ones who do."

If you are naturally creative, you know that creative gifts or imaginative ideas can flow at unexpected times. And at times, not at all.

I was chosen to develop a storyboard design for a project not long ago. With the deadline approaching, I fought to envision the storyline. Concepts would come and then quickly leave. Mentally, I felt like I was trying to create a dust-free zone in a windstorm. The harder my mind worked to clear a spot, the dustier my thoughts became. I had a brain full of ideas and had second thoughts about every one of them. A lack of confidence affected my creativity.

Was I capable of writing anything original? Were my ideas worth sharing? Reaching back for a memory I could use for inspiration; I remembered something my granddaughter created in first grade. The assignment was to create a storyboard for her life from birth to first grade.

As an extraordinarily creative and talented artist, the project was easy for her. As she painted the poster board, I grabbed the supplies she wanted and watched a genuinely original story come to life.

She lined each photo, drawing, sticker, personal item, and hand-drawn art on the table in sequence and glued them to the poster board. First was a picture of herself at birth, then drawings of her cat, her favorite toys, pictures of her family, bracelets she made, and photographs of fun places she had been. My eyes filled with tears when everything was firmly attached to the page.

This seven-year-old had created a compelling masterpiece. While it wasn't a meticulously designed storyboard for a *Star Wars* movie, it showed a natural progression from moment to moment, depicting her journey. Last week I needed inspiration, and I went to the closet to get a fresh look at her storyboard. At that moment, I understood the storyboard for my project didn't need to be perfect, just meaningful.

Maybe you are different, but overthinking can be overwhelming. We can be far more productive once we trust our creative instincts without questioning the outcome. Although it helps not to overthink our work, we do need other eyes on it.

## CRITIQUES AND COLLABORATION

Creative concepts are often the result of collaborative exchange. If we are to create works beyond our individual talents, we must be vulnerable and open to cross-examination.

I know it takes a great deal of courage to place our ideas on the chopping block, but sometimes we need the fat trimmed off our concepts.

I cannot count the number of times I've had to step into an unfamiliar environment and produce ideas that weren't neatly tucked away in my knowledge backpack. I had to cringe through crisis and pull out ways to contribute. Sometimes my thoughts fell flat; other times, those concepts landed million-dollar contracts. Unless we are willing to take risks, we will miss the rewards that come from floating our thoughts into waters that may be over our heads.

Complex problem solving will require a collaborative exchange in a culture where innovation moves faster than imagination.

For those of you who may not be familiar with the inner workings of information technology, many consider it to be the "smoke and mirrors" that happen behind the walls to generate the services we use. Like electricity, information technology is an overlooked commodity.

Most people don't consider the value of those services until the screen goes blank or internal systems go dark.

I remember when my career required that I create an assessment of how information technology would shape our organization's future. The task was daunting, as the presentation included detailed information requiring hours of research. I worked for weeks analyzing data. Somewhere during the data aggregation and digital preparation, I had an epiphany.

As an IT professional, I didn't think the same as most women my age. After so many years in the business, it finally occurred to me that my mind is wired to see problems and solutions that are not obvious to others. The years I spent focusing on planning, security, innovation, and tools for learning allowed me to see what happened in the background.

Working in education helped me spot the gaps between those who controlled the technology and those who used it.

After much deliberation, I decided to share the data results in a visually stimulating way. To drive home the findings, I chose unique jeweled trinkets close to the same size. One was round and smooth, the other square and jagged. My illustration was a catchy and memorable way of explaining the idea of how a square peg could fit into a round hole. There was a gap, and we needed to work together to close it.

As the animated part of my presentation rolled, I asked, "What can we do when we don't see things through the same filter?"

I responded, "We make jewelry."

Everyone in the room laughed, and my boss said, "We love jewelry."

I smiled and began the question-and-answer part of the session. Looking back, I realize that meeting was a huge learning curve in my career. It is not only okay to be original; it is necessary. Although our team approached educational challenges from different perspectives, it took originality from the entire team to create a successful plan. After wrapping up the project, I resolved to work with, rather than against, how I was wired.

### VIEW LIFE AS AN ADVENTURE

We all know those who view life as an adventure. You know … the brave who take life head-on, dive into deep water, and push the envelope daily as they seek their latest quest. We also know those who make an adventure out of everyday life, regardless of location, circumstances, or the status of their dreams.

Growing up, Sunny Anderson's parents relocated to different cities around the world. Rather than resenting the moves, Sunny embraced them.

She chose to view life as an adventure and worked challenges to her advantage. One of the perks of traveling the world at a young age was that Sunny was exposed to different types of cuisine.

Early on, Sunny developed an appreciation for culinary art. After high school, Sunny joined the Air Force and became a journalist and radio broadcaster.

Eventually, Sunny settled in New York City and established a catering business where she prepared dishes that showcased her original flair. In 2005, she was a special guest on the cooking show *Emeril Live*. Recognizing her on-air talents and culinary skills, television executives offered her roles hosting a variety of original network programs, including *Gotta Get It, Cooking For Real, How'd That Get on My Plate? Home Made in America with Sunny Anderson,* and *The Kitchen.*

What could we accomplish if we viewed each season in life as an adventure?

Sunny turned her childhood experiences into successful endeavors that would shape her destiny. Diving into self-discovery and exploring distinctive parts of our personality will lead us to unique opportunities. From famous chef to skilled professionals there is a part of us who wants to break free from the mundane and unleash our uncommon creativity. What stops us from opening our minds and hearts to recognize our gifts and the purpose God intended for us?

### ORIGINALITY IN DIVERSE SETTINGS

Several weeks ago, I read an article about social media curators. Let's face it; the internet can be an overwhelming mess. With so much information available, it's a miracle we find anything at all. If we ask search engines for help, discovering new things can be challenging. Have you ever searched for something simple and had the search engine return thousands of items? Learning the art of refining our keywords can feel like earning a doctoral level college degree. I'm thankful for those who peruse the mountains of information available and provide us with much-needed filters. After all, who doesn't appreciate a list of the top ten latest technology gadgets, popular children's gifts, or top 100 most successful writers?

I admit there are times when I don't want to be precise about what I'm searching for and ask the search engine to give me general information. Last week, in a small group discussion, we talked about the life of King David. Knowing we would be talking about him for weeks to come, I researched all I could on his life and legacy.

As I made my way through historical archives, I caught a glimpse of how courageous David was when he defended his father's flock of sheep from a lion and a bear. I felt his humility when King Saul called on him to soothe his emotional distress.

When Saul felt the presence of evil spirits, he summoned David, and when David sang, the evil spirits departed. Later in life, David would be forced to hide in caves from the king who sought to kill him. It would be years before David would become King of Israel and establish the capital in Jerusalem. During his reign, David made Jerusalem the religious center of the nation. He developed plans to relocate religious artifacts to the city.

Although David desired to build a temple for Jehovah in Jerusalem, God would not allow it. In the book of Chronicles, God instructed the prophet Nathan to tell David, *"Go and tell my servant David, 'Thus says the LORD: It is not you who will build me a house to dwell in"* (1 Chronicles 17:4, ESV). Although God did not give David permission to build the temple, He allowed David's son Solomon to build the majestic edifice.

Solomon spared no expense in his architectural plans for the building. The world's most skilled artists created the temple's architecture and aesthetic designs. Solomon's obedience and wisdom, in tandem with his originality, produced the temple God desired.

Financial analysts estimate that the gold and silver used to construct the temple would be worth approximately 250 billion dollars in today's economy. The Universal Church of the Kingdom of God in Sao Paulo, Brazil, built a 10,000-seat replica of the temple of Solomon several years ago for 300 million dollars. Although it does not include every detail that the original Temple of Solomon had, its blueprint is similar and has many modern luxuries. Solomon's Temple remains one of the top architectural achievements in history.

### BECOMING CHILDLIKE

Maybe you can't create social sites like Grant or possess the culinary skills of Sunny or the architectural abilities of Solomon. Still, you do have gifts that God wants you to use. The circumstances that we have walked through in life are catalysts that unlock our creativity.

Our skills and talents may be different but our calling to creativity is universal. Sometimes we need to take a step back from the day-to-day grind to unlock our imagination.

Maybe that is why millions of adults make Disney World one of their top vacation destinations. There is something restorative about reverting back to an imaginative childlike state that is not held hostage by adulthood.

Can you remember the feeling of freedom you experienced as your hands slid across the paper when you moved a crayon?

You did not expect to stay in the lines; you just drew, allowing multiple colors to become art. Although I'm not an artist, that's the way I felt the first time I held a digital pencil and wrote words on the surface of a tablet while at a conference.

On a long table in front of me were perfectly placed tablets with stunning digital art. A portrait of a United States president caught my eye. When I asked about the picture, I learned it was created by finger-painting on the tablet. The artist's name was Kyle Lambert. An illustrator from Los Angeles is best known for creating incredible movie posters for companies such as Disney, Marvel, Netflix, and Sony Pictures.

Amazingly, most are drawn on tablets with digital pencils. Lambert ingeniously pushed the limit when others didn't see the depth of his vision.

Edwin Land, a scientist, inventor, and co-founder of the Polaroid Corporation, said, "An essential aspect of creativity is not being afraid to fail."

When was the last time you tried to do something that might make you look foolish?

## TAKING RISKS AND TAKING THE NEXT STEP

Many women have risked everything to follow their dreams. Libby Crow was an honor student, prom queen, and star athlete in Wyoming. She attended college and began her adult life as an overworked and underpaid elementary school teacher. At twenty-five, she was dumped by her boyfriend, quit her job, and moved to Denver, Colorado, for a fresh start. Grieving the death of her father, she felt lonely and depressed. One day skimming through social media, Libby reached out to a friend who changed her life forever.

Once Libby committed to personal growth, she created the life she longed to live. Returning to her roots as an educator, she helped clients transform their personal journeys and gave them insights into running successful businesses.

Her work was featured in Forbes, Entrepreneur, ABC, NBC, FOX, CBS, and more. That's impressive for a girl from a small town. By opening up, capitalizing on her originality, and transforming her life, her programs teach skills from social media management to building and structuring online businesses. In addition, she and her husband, Scott Oldford, are co-founders of *The Daily Shift,* a personal development company for entrepreneurs.

We never can foresee what situations we will face in life or become part of determining our success.

However, we know our experiences lead us to forks in the road and times for a decision. No matter what we choose, our choices will guide us through our next trip. The option is like being given a ladder.

What do we do with it? Do we stand on it to see what we cannot see from our current perspective? Do we climb to the other side without knowing what is waiting for us? Or do we leave it where it is and jump the fence or climb the wall?

Don't question your original thoughts. They are part of you. When I struggle for something as small as an original idea, I search for memories that impacted me. Situations turned into successes and words of wisdom shared by those who care for me.

As I ponder those today, I remembered something my grandmother shared with me often. "You were born to be original, don't change who you are for anyone else."

Reflect on your personal journey and remember the transformative words that shaped your life. Write them down and try to commit them to your memory if you need them again.

If you feel pressure to blend in with the crowd, reach back for the words that encouraged you, made you strong, and guided you to be the person you are today.

Never forget you are unique, a one-of-a-kind person with distinctive ideas and unrivaled talents. Use your inspiration to create new perspectives for yourself and others. Pull back from the need to overthink your ideas. Allow yourself to be unconventional; it's the way you were made. And never forget that no matter how much you downplay your life experiences, you have something to share.

Someone needs to hear and live by your words of wisdom. So take a chance and reach out to someone who may not receive wisdom and inspiration. Share a blog post, recommend a book, get a group together and paint, sing, or share a meal. Encourage each other.

Dr. Cindy Trimm said, "That's right. You are a designer's original, a true sight to see. You have to understand that you are not here by mistake and that you were created on purpose and for a purpose. You are something to marvel at."

# Chapter Eleven

# FLEXIBILITY AND RESILIENCE

A FEW YEARS AGO, OUR FRIENDS INVITED US TO VACATION with them in Colorado. After a few days of resting in our rented home, we decided to go white-water rafting. Our guide went over the safety procedures on the bus ride to the rapids and passed out the life jackets. After we grabbed our paddles and climbed into the raft, he told us to listen for the safety signals.

He cautioned us that we would have to work together and pull in the same direction if we were to make it through the snake bend safely.

The first part of the journey was easy. The shallow waters gently pushed our raft forward, and we relaxed in the river's rhythm. Floating along, we went around bends and curves that gave way to magnificent views of mountains and scaled rock formations.

A few miles downstream, David, our guide, raised his hand and signaled for us to paddle. We craned our necks in search of the rapids that lay ahead. Trying to gather our confidence, we stared at David and then at each other. We exchanged awkward looks of excitement, trying to act prepared for the unexpected. As the raft bounced up and down, it gently sprayed the water.

Working together, we paddled through the rapids until the boat made a final bounce and landed in calm water.

An hour into the journey, we took a rest along the shore. After our break, we slid back into the raft for the final leg of our trip. Rounding a few bends, I heard the roar of the water and then saw jagged rocks and sprays of water reaching toward the sky.

My heart pounded as I realized what was coming next. David signaled for us to lean toward the right and prepare to paddle. The front of the raft took a hard dip down, then a shot back up. A wall of water swamped the raft, and it rocked against the current. Pushing and pulling our oars deep into the river, we rowed hard to avoid the rocks.

Although our group had anticipated working hard, we had underestimated the river's strength. When the back of the raft came down and smacked the water, my friend sitting in front of me ended up in my lap. I couldn't paddle, and I couldn't move, and neither could my friend.

The current continued to toss the raft like a toy. When the raft finally came to a rest, we let out long sighs of relief that gave rise to laughter. We didn't notice, but a photographer snapped a picture as we entered the roughest part of the rapids. The image rests against our mantle, a reminder that we can forge our way through the unexpected dips and turns with focus and determination.


PEACE INVADERS

On any given day, our peace can be invaded by minor annoyances or traumatic events that can change our lives forever. Like the rough waters along the rapids, there are days we will have to dig deep and push against the tide of things that would pull us under.

A small, confident eight-year-old girl stood on the wave's edge as her board broke the plane and pointed toward the sea.

The recipient of a significant surfing scholarship at a young age, Bethany Hamilton was destined to be a champion. At age thirteen, tragedy struck when she was attacked by a large tiger shark that amputated her arm below the shoulder. At the hospital, she lost more than sixty percent of her blood; Hamilton's courage kept her alive. She stunned the world by returning to surfing a month after the attack.

Two years later, she won her first national surfing title. In 2017, she was inducted into the Surfers' Hall of Fame. Hamilton's autobiography, *Soul Surfer: A True Story of Faith, Family, and Fighting to Get Back on the Board,* was adapted into the acclaimed film *Soul Surfer.* Although Bethany returned to surfing, she later wrote in a social media post, "13 years ago from today life with one arm began. So many doubts, fears, and unknowns flooded my world ... But the hope I found as a Christian led me to overcome, along with the amazing support of my family, the kindness of my community, and my life's passions." Her resilient attitude brought hope and strength to millions around the world.

Although I have amazing times of courage and resilience, I admit that I also have times when I feel like an NFL Football player running back and forth dodging tackles. When I find myself in those places, I say a quick prayer, remember the ultimate destination, and move toward it.

### RESILIENCE AND CALM

Over the years, I have found that spending time in nature helps my mind untangle twisted thoughts and allows me to let loose of toxic emotions.

While deep-sea fishing in Hawaii, my rod suddenly bent forward. Caught off guard, I rushed to harness myself in the seat and pull the rod back to keep it from breaking. Once the fish was in the boat, the rod straightened, and the line released the tension. Later that night, I thought about how close the line came to snapping.

The fish would have cracked the rod in half if I had not used a weight-bearing line. I pushed forward that image and thought about friends and leaders who found ways to hold on to things that could have easily gotten away.

The ability to be resilient under pressure is a trait we should all long to acquire.

*Resilience* is described as "the ability of a person to adjust or recover readily from illness, adversity, major life changes." Maybe you have a handful of friends that fit that description; I know I do.

I have watched close friends recover from near-death experiences, others rebuild their businesses after financial hardships, and others find reconciliation after betrayal. Like rubber bands, they stretch beyond their size, hold things together, and then, when released, regain their original shape.

One of the most inspiring things about strong-hearted people is their ability to remain calm in the face of disaster. Change and loss are emotions that most of us have to cycle through.

If you have lost a loved one to death, had a close relationship fall apart, or circumstances leave you feeling uncertain, you know the importance of recovering emotionally. Resiliency gives us the psychological strength to cope with stress and adversity. Like a *reservoir* of power, we can find the fortitude to stay mentally strong when our mind tells us to fall apart.

## CONTROLLING YOUR REACTION

Although we can't control life's difficulties, we can control our reactions.

When I was young, a friend bought her son a Batman punching toy. Whenever her son punched it, it went back or over to one side, then immediately sprang back up. Irrespective of how many times he hit the toy, it immediately bounced back.

My friend and I took a few adult swings at Batman, but our attempts failed to keep him down. I am sure you know real-life versions of the bounce-back Batman, those uncommonly resilient people that are brave enough to rebound after brutal attacks. They land on their feet when the earth shifts underneath them. But sometimes, a series of swings will topple the toughest.

Even warriors need a season of rest.

An article revealed that the ability to recover quickly from problematic situations is influenced by self-reflection. Individuals who see themselves as objective tend to remain calm in stressful situations and have an optimistic outlook.

Conversely, individuals who believe that fate, luck, or other people are dominant influences in their lives are less optimistic. The article indicated that whether one views things from an internal or external perspective, each person can discover healthy ways of dealing with stress. The article spoke to me about the importance of social support. It emphasized mentally strong people often have the affirmation of family and friends who offer wisdom and emotional help in difficult times.

## DON'T GO IT ALONE

I cannot count the times my family, friends, bosses, and coworkers helped me through difficult seasons.

Growing up, I was an independent, free-spirited child and was well into my thirties before I became comfortable with asking others for help. Reaching out for assistance didn't come naturally.

I self-sabotaged opportunities because I was too proud to ask others for their input. Like a child struggling to make it from one side of the pool to the other, I refused to call for help. A few times, my ego kept me from attaining a perfect 4.0.

On another occasion, my drive for perfection drove my closest friend away.

If we are not careful, our pride to go-it-alone can distance us from the people we need most. A verse in the book of Romans underscores our need to be interdependent,

> *"For just as in one [physical] body we have many parts, and these parts do not all have the same function or special use, so we, who are many, are [nevertheless just] one body in Christ, and individually [we are] parts one of another [mutually dependent on each other]"* (Romans 12:4-5 AMP).

Let those words sink into your soul. Whether we are in seasons of success or times of testing, we need each other. We were not created to walk around lost and lonely. My grandchildren understand the need to stick together, and not go it alone.

Our grandchildren looked forward to racing their friends through the local corn maze in the fall. It was more than an outing; it was a full-on quest to conquer the maze and dominate the other teams.

Our tribe divided up the tasks and conducted mock run-through practices the week before the contest. Evan's job was to discover the code that would interface with the maze website. Bryce was in charge of the map and marking the turns and intersections as they moved forward. Paige tested the GPS on her phone to identify emergency exits in case they became lost.

I couldn't help but smile as they planned and prepared. They understood they had a better chance of winning by working together rather than alone. Their planning efforts paid off, and they won first place. While other teams fell apart and blamed each other, their team pulled together and pushed through the complex parts.

## THE MARKS OF RESILIENT PEOPLE

I am sure we can all think of people who somehow found the strength to overcome unthinkable circumstances.

Maybe you know of someone who lived through a catastrophic hurricane or tornado or survived the heartache of the 9/11 tragedy.

Most of us can pull up vivid memories of people standing in the middle of debris or rubble while vowing to rebuild their lives. I can call to mind the image of a family huddled together days after Hurricane Laura. The dad leaned against a pile of splintered wood and pointed to a waist-high pile of their family's belongings and said, "This is all we have left of our past, and we are taking it into our future. We will rebuild ... better than before."

I am amazed that some of the bravest words ever spoken slip off the lips of those standing in the middle of an emotional storm.

Resilient people are usually good communicators and view themselves as fighters rather than victims. I know we've talked about emotional intelligence before, but managing emotions effectively is crucial for the recovery process. Learning to think before we act is one of the best things we can do for ourselves and others.

Resilient people tend to look at situations from a realistic point of view. They accept responsibility for their actions and stay focused on the task before them. By reframing their thoughts, they can solve problems and make changes without blaming others or being swept away by their emotions.

Damon Redd woke up early and went downstairs to find his home and business covered in five feet of mud and water. As he walked down toward the bottom of the stairs, he felt the murky water cover his feet and slowly rise toward his knees. In a dream-like state, Damon slowly surveyed the damage. During the night, flash floods unexpectedly filled the Colorado basin. Overnight, Damon lost *Kind Design,* the business he had spent five years building, his home, and his livelihood. It was the hardest thing he had ever faced.

Damon found an unsuspecting lifeline standing in what could have been the graveyard of his business. Beneath the rubble, he found a box of hats he had ordered (a few months earlier). On the caps were the *Kind Design* logo, a snowflake with a drop of water.

On a whim, he posted the hats on social media. Instantly, they sold out. In the following weeks, Damon sold enough pre-orders to salvage his company. Refusing to be overwhelmed by things outside of his control, he discovered something that could turn a horrible situation into a hope-filled one. It is easy for our thoughts to linger on what we have lost rather than what we have left in crisis situations. In doing so, we often miss the diamond hidden in the dirt.

## SPEAKING LIFE

One of my favorite films is *Wonder*. Based on a bestselling children's novel, it conveys the power of kindness and generosity.

The author R. J. Palacio said, "A decade ago, I was in front of an ice cream store with my two sons. My younger son, who was only three at the time, saw a little girl that had a very significant craniofacial difference. He got a little scared, and he started to cry. In my haste to shield her from seeing his response or his reaction to her face, I whisked him away really quickly. That just got me thinking about what it must be like to face a world every day that doesn't quite know how to face you back."

Palacio said the real-life Mom moment led her to write the bestseller with the message of *Choosing Kind*. Although she had never written a book, *Choosing Kind* sold more than eight million copies worldwide.

The book's theme centers on the main character, Auggie Pullman, who was born with facial differences caused by a rare genetic condition. As a result of the condition, Auggie endured numerous surgeries and multiple hospital stays.

In middle school, he faced many of the same issues as his classmates, but his appearance made him a target for bullying. Although Auggie faced great emotional hardship, his family helped him find inner courage and confidence. The movie underscores milestones in Auggie's journey, including developing friendships, winning the science fair, and conquering his fears as a group of older students start a fight with him.

Along the way, he learned the importance of caring for his emotional health. He discovered ways to help others become comfortable with people who may look or act differently than themselves. The movie concluded with a ceremony at his fifth-grade graduation with Auggie winning a school award for his character and fortitude to push through adversity.

Watching *Wonder* had a profound impact on our granddaughters. After viewing the film together, we walked out of the cinema full of emotions and a deep sense of commitment to speak words of life to others.

Auggie's life positively influenced everyone around him, something we should all strive to do.

## BREAKING UP PROBLEMS INTO BITE-SIZED PIECES

Current social, political, and economic events have created a culture where most of us have leaned in to evaluate what is essential in our lives.

Separated from our jobs, loved ones, and normal daily activities have created a worldwide mental health crisis. More than ever, emphasis has been placed on taking care of our minds and bodies. Core foundations of self-care include prayer, journaling, and focusing on positive things in our lives.

Even when we experience difficult times, it is essential to remain thankful for blessings we often take for granted.

Change is a part of life. Mandy Hale once said, "Growth is painful. Change is painful. But nothing is as painful as staying stuck somewhere you don't belong."

Trying to mask pain or challenges is like putting a piece of gum in the wall of a dam and expecting it to stop a leak. Those small leaks often go unnoticed until the pressure builds, stone shatters, and the water flows out, destroying everything in its path.

Consider times when you have allowed a fleeting thought of fear to weaken your resolve. We've faced a tidal wave of change in the past few years, where finding adjustable strategies can increase our resolve. Sometimes we have to plunge into the waters of change and do some aquatic acrobatics.

Can you think of a problem you can break down into manageable pieces and work toward resolving? If we can successfully redirect our focus to what we can control, we can see beyond what holds us back and push forward in a transformative way.

## BIBLICAL WAYS TO OVERCOME ADVERSITY

The Bible uses a variety of stories, metaphors, and illustrations to highlight ways we can push through adversity and experience positive transformation.

The book of Acts describes how Paul was transformed from a pious religious leader into a merciful follower of Christ. The writer recounts the journey of Paul being attacked by civil mobs, publicly assaulted, unjustly incarcerated, and eventually beheaded by Rome.

One of the redeeming qualities of Paul was that even in persecution, he extended mercy to his enemies. In a letter to his followers at Corinth, he wrote: *"We are afflicted in every way, but not crushed; perplexed, but not driven to despair; persecuted, but not forsaken; struck down, but not destroyed"* (2 Corinthians, 4:8-9 ESV).

Even though your situation may not mirror Paul's, I am sure you have felt the crushing pressure of being misjudged.

What we do in times of adversity influences our future and those following in our footsteps. Even though Paul's earthly journey ended at a guillotine, his resolve to live mercifully filtered through his followers, and that spirit was carried throughout the earth. Even in difficult seasons, don't fail to understand the power of influence you have on those watching your life.

Your journey may be the inspiration someone needs to raise their hand for help, or the strength one borrows in times of crisis. Remember, our journeys mesh together. We are healthier and happier when we can pull hope from each other.

## OPENING OURSELVES TO CHANGE

In the business world, flexible thinking and adaptability are necessary attributes. The other day I heard a colleague share this story: A frog was born in the bottom of a well.

Knowing no different environment, the frog formed its world around the walls of the well. One day, a boy came along, lifted the frog out of the well, and placed him in an open field. Once the frog saw the world more broadly, its limited view was replaced by a more realistic, global perspective.

Like the frog, our mindsets are shaped by our environment and experiences.

One of our friends had a construction company that catered to the local petrochemical market. Because he only dealt with state-wide contractors, he had a limited perspective of how his business could function globally.

After working with national and international consultants, he gained a competitive advantage and expanded his corporation into global markets.

If we are to evolve individually or in our respective career paths, we must remain open to change. I remember a quote a college professor used as an icebreaker to start every class,

> "Progress is impossible without change, and those who cannot change their minds cannot change anything" — George Bernard Shaw.

We often treat our dreams and visions like ships stuck in the harbor. They may look beautiful and well protected while tied to the dock, but ships weren't created to be stared at; they were designed to sail in the open water.

Our dreams were not meant to be carried in our creative wombs forever. At some point, we have to release our dreams and allow them to breathe on their own.

As I write this chapter, the theme of learning to be resilient speaks to my soul deeply and richly. As I think back over the years, I regret missed opportunities to help others work their way through tough times.

I realize if I had taken my eyes off myself more, the Holy Spirit would have shown me the deep needs of others who were within my reach. I hope that committing to reclaim those lost opportunities will position me to find new ones.

Have there been times that you felt you missed a chance to love or support someone? Did your lack of confidence keep you from reaching out, or did your pride keep you at arm's length? Amazingly, we can think of one thousand reasons not to take a chance, when usually all we need is a slight push to step out in faith. I admit it is easy to derail our success by discounting our worth and shelving our God-given talents and abilities.

Today, I made a list of the most challenging times in my life.

I highlighted desperate times of loss, times of great stress, and times when I questioned my abilities and the abilities of others. At the end of each item, I stopped to think about how I pushed forward.

My heart almost melted when I realized there was not a single time when someone didn't step forward and help me. Sometimes generosity and empathy came in the form of a hug, other times in the way of heart-to-heart conversation, and even a message that wasn't comfortable for me to hear.

I encourage you to inventory your life. Call to mind moments when you found the courage to climb out of dark situations or times when you took on the heartache of others. If we allow ourselves to be flexible and open to new opportunities, we can change our lives and the lives of others.

Perhaps the Emperor in Disney's *Mulan* has the right idea: "The flower that blooms in adversity is the rarest and most beautiful."

Each of us are like flowers; strong, beautiful, and resilient.

*Chapter Twelve*

# DETERMINATION

M Y HUSBAND IS A RISK-TAKER WHO PASSIONATELY RAC-
es through life exploring new things. I'm also a risk-taker,
but I like to think things through and have a backup plan
handy. One of our favorite activities is exploring unmarked trails on
our all-terrain vehicle (ATV). When we go on ATV outings, we make
sure the most experienced riders are at the front and rear of the line,
and when the weather conditions are volatile, we pack all-weather gear.

As we entered a logging road, a large cow wandered across our
path. My husband, Gene, who was ahead of us, swerved to miss hitting the cow. When he turned his ATV, it slid across loose gravel and
he lost control. The sharp turn threw him off the ATV and he landed
on the ground.

As I watched the accident, my heart sank. Unsure of what the
scene would look like up close, I stopped my ATV and ran toward him.

After a few minutes, he slowly pulled himself from the ground.
When I realized he wasn't severely injured, I brushed tears from my
eyes and thanked God he was going to recover. It was a wake-up call

for us to be more aware of dangers that might unexpectedly cross our paths.

Years after the accident we journeyed to a mountainous region of Arkansas. The terrain offered trail options that were graded by the level of difficulty. As we approached the park entrance and unloaded the ATVs from the trailer onto the trail, I noticed a sign that said, *Level 1.* Just to be safe we started our journey there.

We quickly discovered that the paths were not like the smooth logging roads. The backwood trails were laced with long limbs, climbing vines, and complicated root systems. To muddy matters, the ground was soaked from the storm that had blown through the area the night before. As we rode through the mud, we intentionally slung it on each other.

Nothing quite like grown-ups playing in the mud.

Later in the ride, we came across a flooded riverbed and our lead rider crossed first. Hesitantly, Dennis made his way through, occasionally rocking his vehicle back and forth to gain traction. Other riders followed his lead and made it across too. When it was my turn to cross the raging river, I froze. My heart raced at the thought of trekking across the slippery rocks and I imagined a dozen negative scenarios. After a lengthy wait, I traversed the river and made it to the other side.

Once I was settled, my dad pulled up beside me and asked, "What took you so long?"

We laughed but I knew he was right; I had waited too long and should have trusted my instincts and riding ability.

On the way back, we ventured down a trail that appeared to be dry. Somehow in the excitement, we missed the sign that showed a higher level of difficulty. At first, everything was beautiful, but then the high degree of complexity presented a new set of challenges.

A few miles in we pulled to a stop. On the left side was a deep ravine and on the right side was a fifteen-foot rock wall. We studied the trail map and from the grade of the lines, we realized that steep terrain was ahead. Dennis climbed a steep knoll and then reached a flat spot at the top. As his wheels caught the edge, he rotated the throttle and the ATV disappeared. We waited several moments and then saw him standing at the top of the hill.

When my turn came, I focused on the top of the incline, not the slippery mud beneath me. I made it to the point where Dennis said to go straight but didn't see a rock hidden by the tall grass. My ATV hit the rock and came to a complete stop. The sudden jolt crushed the handlebars into the right side of my chest. I went ahead and made my way to the top then went back to the trail to warn other riders of the hidden danger.

Knowing my dad's ATV did not have four-wheel drive, our friend Raymond offered to switch ATVs with him.

With a bit of persuading, my dad agreed. As Raymond started up the hill, the incline was too much for the ATV. It flipped over, slid down the trail, and fell on its side with Raymond underneath it. From the top of the hill, the men ran to pull the ATV off of him. Although he could stand up, his arms and hands were bleeding. One of our group grabbed the first aid kit and wrapped him in bandages.

Unable to continue, we journeyed back to the cabins. On the drive back, I noticed a large scrape and gash on the side of Raymond's helmet. Without the helmet, our friend would have been seriously injured. While riding back in silence, we thanked God he had only minor cuts and bruises. Along the way, I noticed the trail marker said, *Level 3—for experienced riders only.*

Once again, we had defied the odds and escaped without serious injury.

Determined to conquer the mountain and our fears, the next day we attacked each stage of the trek with relentless resolve. Completing the most challenging trail was euphoric. Gathered together we stood on top of the mountain and soaked in the 360-degree view.

Challenging ourselves to venture through the tough terrain was worth the journey and the view.

## ENCOUNTERING CHALLENGES OF DIFFERENT DIFFICULTY LEVELS

I'm sure you've had hills to climb and fears to face.

Unfortunately, we can't always pick the difficulty levels for the trials we face. If we want to cross the finish line there will be times when we must gather ourselves, pray, and push forward.

Our difficulties may not always be found in exciting activities or moments when we wrestle with ourselves to overcome challenges. Sometimes our biggest undertakings hide in our communications. While walking through the neighborhood last week, I saw a family walking down the path, laughing, talking, and enjoying their time together.

Taking in their joy, my husband and I waved as we walked past them. Further down the path, I noticed a father and daughter walking together but they were not interacting. The father was walking about six feet in front of his daughter, and she was staring at her phone.

I thought about how easy it is to lose sight of the most important relationships in our lives. In our media-cluttered culture it takes intentional effort not to lose sight of the relations that matter most; including our relationship with our family and with God.

I've always been inspired by those who overcome great adversity and stay true to their goals and dreams.

Several years ago, I read an inspirational piece highlighting Alex's Lemonade Stand Foundation (ALSF). Alex Scott was diagnosed with neuroblastoma shortly before her first birthday.

Alex's doctors told her parents that even if she were to beat cancer that she would never walk again. Despite the negative report, the Scotts continued to encourage Alex to move her legs, and with great determination, Alex began to crawl and then used braces to stand up before age two. For more than a year she continued to progress and defy the odds. Her story took another serious turn when the doctors discovered more tumors throughout her body.

Even with the challenging report, Alex was determined to fight forward. While in the hospital, Alex told her mom that she wanted a lemonade stand so that she could raise money to help other kids like her.

True to her dream, her first lemonade stand raised $2,000 for the hospital. Although Alex passed away at age eight, her dream continued, and others helped raise over $1 million for cancer research. Years later, the picture of Alex smiling behind a lemonade stand lingers in my mind.

Her determination and love for others launched a foundation that is making a difference in the lives of those who experience great suffering.

## LOOKING FOR INSPIRATION

I am sure you have a list of people who have greatly inspired you. If you were to write out the positive attributes of those on your list, *determination* would probably be a common characteristic. Now take a moment and revise that list to include you.

If your friends, family, or colleagues were asked to describe your best traits, would *determination* be on their list? Would you use that attribute to describe yourself?

Wouldn't it be wonderful if we could journey through life without being weighed down by discouragement and disappointment? When I feel like struggles are beginning to sabotage my dreams, I look for inspiration from those who overcame great odds to accomplish their goals.

Just last week I read a post that revealed that Michael Jordan was cut from his high school basketball team his sophomore year. It's hard to imagine, but it's true.

Although Jordan could have allowed the rejection to defeat him, he worked hard and became a legendary player in the NBA. Michael

Jordan attributes his success to learning from his failures. Jordan once said,

> "I have missed more than 9,000 shots in my career. I have lost almost 300 games. On 26 occasions, I have been entrusted to take the game-winning shot and missed. I have failed over and over and over again in my life. And that is why I succeed."

Determination and grit can turn our daydreams into our destiny.

If you haven't experienced the exhilaration of overcoming a challenging situation, hang on. I am sure life will give you more than one chance to turn adversity into opportunity. Consider the people you know, who have suffered setbacks and turned them into great successes. What inspiration do you find in their success stories?

When I read through the Bible, I am mindful that most of the legendary men and women had complicated backstories.

Men like Moses were born under a death threat. When we read about his life, it is easy to skip right over the part where the leader of the nation made it illegal to give birth to a male Hebrew child. Let's push that thought forward and consider the faith his mother had to defy such an order. From the moment of conception, Moses' life and destiny were fought over. That kind of tension doesn't make life easy, but it can turn average into exceptional, and common into extraordinary. Moses' life probably didn't mirror the Moses portrayed in most Bible movies.

His story wasn't some slick montage of epic-filled moments.

What some Bible narratives fail to communicate is the humanity of larger-than-life leaders. Just like most leaders in our culture, Moses sometimes failed.

There were times when his humanity seeped into the story and history records those moments right alongside the miracle. He had anger issues and even murdered a man prior to his conversion. Even after God raised him up to be a leader of Israel, he still made grave mistakes. One severe mess-up kept him out of the promised land altogether.

But even in his humanity, Moses was determined to follow God. He knew his calling was to deliver a nation out of slavery and into freedom. That grit and determination to obey God transformed a murderer into a global leader.

## BECOMING A WORLD CHANGER

Like Moses, God is calling on us to use our faith and determination to be world-changers. And if we are to answer that call, we must dive deep into His word, leaning in so we can hear His voice.

Our world needs us to stand up and demonstrate the love of Christ. Each of us knows someone who is lonely, hurting, or struggling to find the truth.

God has graced us with His love so that we can reach the lost, restore the broken, and mentor the marginalized. If you aren't sure how to show the love of Christ, pray and ask. God will give you the wisdom, strength, and courage to lead others away from destruction and into purpose.

If you need a verse on courage, I encourage you to read and memorize this passage: *"Be strong and courageous! Do not be terrified or dismayed (intimidated), for the LORD your God is with you wherever you go"* (Joshua 1:9, AMP).

## COMMIT EVERYTHING TO PRAYER

When situations threaten our peace, it is easy for our thoughts to flow in a negative direction. I would be overwhelmed if I added up all the times that my mind pushed my emotions over the edge. I admit that I've acted in ways that I deeply regret because my mind uncorked bottled-up emotions.

Had I stepped back and prayed first, things might have ended differently.

I attended a management training session that focused on the book *The Seven Habits of Highly Effective People* by Stephen Covey. Covey described one's Circle of Concern as the wide variety of concerns others have for their family, health, job, and global issues.

Reactive people focus their efforts in the Circle of Concern by concentrating on the problems and circumstances they have no control over. The training session explained that our Circle of Influence is defined by the areas that we feel we have some level of influence or control over. Proactive people focus on the Circle of Influence by working on situations they can change.

Truthfully, we cannot control people or circumstances. Sometimes the best approach is to manage what is in our reach and commit the unresolved issues to prayer and God.

## CIRCLING BACK ON THE JOURNEY

As we prepare to close out this chapter, I think of the journey I've made this year. I've experienced many memorable moments and a few low places, and I am sure you have too. That is the beautiful part of self-discovery, we have the opportunity to pull out undiscovered courage. To push beyond our comfort zone and challenge ourselves to dream bigger dreams.

Pulling from my personal notes from when I started writing this manuscript:

> *As I sit here looking out the window, searching for words that I know aren't going to come quickly, I wonder what I could say about striving to reach the top of the glass ceiling and pave the way for others; or about pushing to have the perfect marriage, and perfect children … I don't want to recount meaningless conversations or recall things that aren't relevant. But I do want to help answer the questions that*

*are on women's minds and I want us to build authentic relationships with each other. Which means I have to lean in and listen. How do people feel? What are they saying? How can I help a sister who feels like she isn't enough or doesn't have the strength to stay the course? I want honest conversation, nothing shallow or superficial. I want to pull the covers back and uncover what we have been hiding from each other. I'm not sure what I can say but I trust God will give me the words.*

As we circle back through the journey, we discovered that many of our struggles and emotions are linked to our actions and reactions. We also found that we have a tendency to cling to what is comfortable rather than trying something new. Truthfully, we know the importance of self-care, emotional equity, and healthy boundaries but sometimes we struggle to make them a priority.

While conducting interviews with accomplished women, I noticed the inner struggles that hide behind their successes. I don't like admitting that when I asked them to describe their qualifications or speak about a time when they achieved a milestone or accomplishments that they shrank back and were apprehensive.

I've done that; I am sure you have too. It is common for a thread of fear to unravel our cloak of confidence.

If you have snagged your favorite sweater, you know that one thread doesn't usually unravel all the fabric, just a section. But what if you tried to use scissors to fix the snag and then end up with a hole? Similarly, confidence doesn't usually disappear because of a snag. But if we keep cutting a tear eventually there will be a gaping hole.

The same truth can be applied to our courage. If we are not careful, the tear of unforgiveness, doubt, fear, or anxiety will unravel our courage. If we are to maximize our time and talents, we must guard our courage.

For a moment, I want you to lay aside what the world is saying about you. Forget about the opinions of your friends and family.

Push past what your co-workers are telling you and stop comparing your life with someone else's social media feed. Put all that out of the way and use your first-person voice to read what God says about you:

I am God's child. (John 1:12)

I am accepted. (Romans 15:7)

I am God's work of art, created to do good works. (Ephesians 2:10)

I am not condemned. (Romans 8:1)

I am complete in Christ. (Colossians 2:10)

I have peace through God who guards my mind and heart. (Philippians 4:7)

I have wisdom, righteousness, and redemption in Jesus. (1 Corinthians 1:30)

I am no longer a slave to sin. (Romans 6:6)

I am set free from sin and death. (Romans 8:2)

I am a joint heir with Christ. (Romans 8:17)

I am predestined by God to obtain an inheritance. (Ephesians 1:11)

I hope you read through that list twice because that is how your Father feels about you. If you can't believe all of these words, choose one verse. Read it over multiple times, let the words wash over your mind, and pray those words over your future.

Most importantly, *believe them* and have the self-confidence to share them with others.

I will leave you with this thought; in the film *The Princess Diaries,* The Princess of Genovia received this advice from her father on her sixteenth birthday: "Courage is not the absence of fear, but rather the judgment that something else is more important than fear. The brave may not live forever, but the cautious do not live at all. From now on you'll be traveling the road between who you think you are and who you can be. The key is to allow yourself to make the journey."

Whether you are twenty-five or eighty-five those words are for you too. Grasp them. Share them. Live them.

# NOTES

**CHAPTER ONE**

"Too Many People Stay In Bad Relationships, New Survey Says,
And Here's Why." Bustle. Last modified November 30, 2015.
https://www.bustle.com/articles/126572-too-many-people-
stay-in-bad-relationships-new-survey-says-and-heres-why.

"Trigger." Www.dictionary.com. Accessed October 25, 2022.
https://www.dictionary.com/browse/trigger.

Bevere, John. *The Bait of Satan, 20th Anniversary Edition: Living Free from the Deadly Trap of Offense.* Charisma Media,
2014, p.7.

"Avalanche." Encyclopedia Britannica. Accessed October 25, 2022.
https://www.britannica.com/science/avalanche.

"5 Benefits of Healthy Relationships _ Northwestern Medicine."
Scribd. Accessed October 25, 2022. https://www.scribd.
com/document/519208951/5-Benefits-of-Healthy-Relation-
ships-Northwestern-Medicine.

**CHAPTER TWO**

Brown, Brené. *Daring Greatly: How the Courage to be Vulnerable*

*Transforms the Way We Live, Love, Parent, and Lead.* Portfolio, 2015, p. 51.

Adams, Bailey. "The Busy Person's Guide to the Done List." I Done This. Accessed October 25, 2022. https://app.idonethis.com/ docs/The-Busy-Persons-Guide-to-the-Done-List.pdf.

*The Hunger Games.* Directed by Francis Lawrence and Gary Ross. 2012. Lionsgate, Film.

## CHAPTER THREE

*Fantastic Four.* Directed by Tim Story. 2005. 20th Century Fox, Film.

*Catfish.* Directed by Henry Joost and Ariel Schulman Henry Joost and Ariel Schulman. 2010. Universal Pictures, Film.

"The Symbiotic Crocodile-Plover Friendship." Rose Wadenya Books. Accessed October 25, 2022. https://www.rosewadenya-books.com/blog/the-symbiotic-crocodile-plover-friendship.

"5 Record Breaking Gemstones Even Billionaires Can't Buy." MINING.COM. Last modified February 25, 2018. https://www.mining.com/web/5-record-breaking-gemstones-even-billionaires-cant-buy.

"The World's Largest Emerald - Colombia, Zambia, Brazil, Austria - Video." *Gemic.* 1. April 16, 2021. https://gem.agency/the-worlds-largest-emerald/.

"How Diamonds Are Formed." Cape Town Diamond Museum. Last modified November 22, 2011. https://www.capetowndiamondmuseum.org/about-diamonds/formation-of-diamonds/.

Shelton, Trent. "Rehab Time." *YouTube.* 1. January 7, 2013. https://www.youtube.com/watch?v=frJS6fJEtVM&list=PLVqBqA-a0xYxS_4zRcu1ni5UQrnv3_O5wx.

Shelton, Trent. "You Deserve Better,." *YouTube.* 1. March 13, 2013. https://www.youtube.com/ watch?v=aX1-N8Nu9Rk.


CHAPTER FOUR

Reshma Saujani, "Teach Girls Bravery, Not Perfection," TED: Ideas Worth Spreading. Accessed October 25, 2022. https://www. ted.com/talks/reshma_saujani_teach_girls_bravery_not_perfection?language=en.

Girls Who Code. "Missing Code." *YouTube.* 1. December 7, 2020. Missing Code." YouTube. Last modified December 7, 2020. https://www.youtube.com/watch?v=bmA45AMqVK4.

"The Most Common Phobias From A to Z." Verywell Mind. Last modified December 16, 2005. https://www.verywellmind. com/list-of-phobias-2795453.

"This is Khalida Popal | Hummel.net." Hummel®. Accessed October 25, 2022. https://www.hummel.net/khalida-popal.html.

"The Dangerous Life Of A Female Football Player In Afghanistan." HuffPost UK. Last modified July 29, 2016. https://www. huffingtonpost.co.uk/entry/khalida-popal-afghanistan-womens-football-team_uk_579b2de2e4b07cb01dcf72b1.

"Esther." Catholic Answers. Last modified November 19, 2018. https://www.catholic.com/encyclopedia/esther.

"Just a Moment..." Just a Moment... Accessed October 25, 2022. https://www.encyclopedia.com/philosophy-and-religion/ bible/old-testament/esther#:~:text=Persian%20Queen%20Esther%20(492%20B.C.,empire%20in%20the%20known%20 world.

"Empowered/." Empowered Wiki. Accessed October 25, 2022. https://empowered.fandom.com/wiki/Empowered/.

"Mary Barra: The 100 Most Influential People of 2021." Time. Last modified September 15, 2021. https://time.com/collection/100-most-influential-people-2021/6095976/mary-barra/.

"What Animals Tell Us About Female Leadership." BBCpage. Accessed October 25, 2022. https://www.bbc.com/worklife/article/20180925-with-females-in-charge-bonobo-society-is-more-chilled-out.

## CHAPTER FIVE

"Need For Significance, Why Feeling Significant is Important." Tonyrobbins.com. Last modified May 15, 2018. https://www.tonyrobbins.com/personal-growth/need-for-significance/.

"Eugene Lang, Investor Who Made College Dreams a Reality, Dies at 98 (Published 2017)." The New York Times - Breaking News, US News, World News and Videos. Last modified April 10, 2017. https://www.nytimes.com/2017/04/08/nyregion/eugene-lang-dead-harlem-college.html.

"Founders Online: Advice to a Young Tradesman, [21 July 1748]." Founders Online. Accessed October 25, 2022. https://founders.archives.gov/documents/Franklin/01-03-02-0130.

Colan, Lee. "How to Go From Being Successful to Being Significant." Inc.com. Last modified July 29, 2015. https://www.inc.com/lee-colan/how-to-move-from-success-to-significance.html.

"Positive Daily Affirmations: Is There Science Behind It?" PositivePsychology.com. Last modified July 29, 2020. https://positivepsychology.com/daily-affirmations/.

Howell, Elizabeth. "How Long Would It Take to Cross the Milky Way at Light Speed?" Livescience.com. Last modified July 3, 2018. https://www.livescience.com/62977-how-big-is-milky-way.html.

"World Population Clock: 7.98 Billion People (2022)." Worldometer - Real Time World Statistics. Accessed October 25, 2022. https://www.worldometers.info/world-population.

"Elizabeth Blackwell: First Woman Physician in America." ThoughtCo. Last modified January 23, 2007. https://www.thoughtco.com/elizabeth-blackwell-biography-3528555/.

Mitchell, Tracey. *Becoming Brave: How to Think Big, Dream Wildly, and Live Fear-Free.* Nashville: Thomas Nelson, 2018. p. 33.

## CHAPTER SIX

Team USA. "Kerri Strug Perseveres To Win Gold | Gold Medal Moments Presented By HERSHEY'S." *YouTube.* 1. June 14, 2018. https://www.youtube.com/watch?v=7VzDDLumYYU.

Bill. "The Keys to Her Success? Core Values, Empathy, Dreams and Energy!" Branding For Results. Last modified September 5, 2018. https://brandingforresults.com/angela-ahrendts/.

"Get "Energized" at HGB's 6th Annual Gala." My AL!VE |. Accessed October 25, 2022. https://www.myalive.com/news-events/stories/get-%E2%80%9Cenergized%E2%80%9D-hg-b%E2%80%99s-6th-annual-gala.

"My Father's Voice." LinkedIn. Last modified June 16, 2017. https://www.linkedin.com/pulse/my-fathers-voice-angela-ahrendts.

Eric Segal. "Leaders and Employees are Burning Out at Record Rates: New Survey, Segal, Edward. "Leaders And Employees Are Burning Out At Record Rates: New Survey." Forbes. Last modified February 17, 2021. https://www.forbes.com/sites/edwardsegal/2021/02/17/leaders-and-employees-are-burning-out-at-record-rates-new-survey/?sh=7541305e6499.

Pegues, Deborah S. *Lead Like a Woman: Gain Confidence, Navi-*

*gate Obstacles, Empower Others.* Harvest House Publishers, 2020. p. 107.

TEDxYouth. "Addicted to Making A Difference: Lauren Selman at TEDxYouth@SantaMonica." *YouTube.* 1. January 13, 2013. https://www.youtube.com/watch?v=1ScJ6Ry6Ucs.

Olympics. "Kerri Strug's Unforgettable Determination to Win Gymnastics Olympic Gold | Strangest Moments." *You-Tube.* 1. January 17, 2018. https://www.youtube.com/watch?v=O4um3YEX51k&list=RDLVbTN_36pn11Q&start_radio=1&rv=bTN_36pn11Q.

Kay, Katty, and Claire Shipman. "The Confidence Gap." The Atlantic. Last modified August 26, 2015. https://www.theatlantic.com/magazine/archive/2014/05/the-confidence-gap/359815.

TEDxTalks. "Confidence: What Does It Do? | Richard Petty | TEDxOhioStateUniversity." *YouTube.* 1. March 16, 2015. https://www.youtube.com/watch?v=cKu-32iyHs0.

Forbes. Accessed October 25, 2022. https://www.forbes.com/sites/ellevate/2019/12/23/secrets-to-confidence-for-every-woman-leader/?sh=44f6f0c36fde.

Cortel, Jason. "Increase Your Emotional Equity by Investing Time in Relationship Building." Jason Cortel. Last modified September 12, 2020. https://www.jasoncortel.com/tuesday-tip-build-emotional-equity/.

CHAPTER SEVEN

Kevin J. Donaldson Quotes (Author of 10 Secrets of the New Rich)." Goodreads | Meet Your Next Favorite Book. Accessed October 25, 2022. https://www.goodreads.com/author/quotes/6909637.Kevin_J_Donaldson.

"All SHERYL SANDBERG Quotes about "Accomplishment"."

inspiringquotes.us. n.d. https://www.inspiringquotes.us/author/5795-sheryl-sandberg/.

"Expecations - the real happiness killer." Accessed October 25, 2022. https://humanpsychology.com.au/expectations-the-real-hapiness-killer/.

*No Time To Die*. Directed by Cary Joji Fukunaga. 2021. Universal Pictures, Film.

"You Can't Hide on Survivor/The Devil You Do or the Devil You Don't." *Survivor.* Directed by Michael Christopher White . CBS, April 13, 2021.

Raypole, Crystal. "Nocebo Effect: When Negative Thinking Impacts Health." Healthline. Accessed October 25, 2022. https://www.healthline.com/health/nocebo-effect.

"Santa Rosa Neighbors Thank Shirley White for Fire Heroics." Santa Rosa Press Democrat. Last modified March 26, 2020. https://www.pressdemocrat.com/article/news/smith-neighbors-thank-shirley-white-for-helping-save-their-homes/.

"HULDAH, Bible Prophetess in Israel Unlocks Secret of Ancient Scroll." Women In The Bible. Last modified November 2, 2018. https://www.womeninthebible.net/women-bible-old-new-testaments/huldah.

"Do You Expect Too Much From Yourself?" Psychology Today. Last modified January 14, 2016. https://www.psychologytoday.com/us/blog/intimacy-path-toward-spirituality/201601/do-you-expect-too-much-yourself.

Got Talent Global. "ERIC CHIEN! The GREATEST Magician Audition EVER On America's Got Talent 2019? | Got Talent." *YouTube.* 1. June 7, 2019. https://www.youtube.com/watch?v=GY7LIjgmX5w.

"Self-Fulfilling Prophecy in Psychology: 10 Examples and Definition (+PDF)." PositivePsychology.com. Last modified January 27, 2022. https://positivepsychology.com/self-fulfilling-prophecy/.

History.com Editors. "New York Yankees' Don Larsen Pitches Only World Series Perfect Game." HISTORY. Last modified September 1, 2021. https://www.history.com/this-day-in-history/don-larsen-world-series-perfect-games-no-hitters.

McGuire, Saundra. "Metacognition: The Key to Producing Brain Based Learning." Lily Conference, Miami University. Accessed October 25, 2022. https://sites01.lsu.edu/faculty/smcgui1/wp-content/uploads/sites/17/2013/11/Lilly-Conference-Miami-University.pdf.

"Women Entrepreneurs Statistics." Find Best Law Jobs in the US in 2022. Last modified February 2, 2021. https://legaljobs.io/blog/women-entrepreneurs-statistics/.

Woods, Laura. "15 Legendary Ways People Struck It Rich." Yahoo Finance - Stock Market Live, Quotes, Business & Finance News. Last modified September 12, 2019. https://finance.yahoo.com/news/15-legendary-ways-people-struck-090000774.html?fr=sycsrp_catchall.

"Rediff.com." Stories on Lifestyle, Fashion, Health and Fitness, Travel. Accessed October 25, 2022. https://getahead.rediff.com/report/2010/apr/26/achievers-jk-rowling-address-to-harvard-grads.html.

"Candy Lightner of MADD (Mothers Against Drunk Driving)." Alcohol Problems and Solutions. Last modified January 16, 2022. https://www.alcoholproblemsandsolutions.org/candy-lightner/.

"30 Motivational Brian Tracy Quotes That Will Change Your Life." Project Life Mastery. Last modified October 4, 2020. https://projectlifemastery.com/brian-tracy-quotes/.

## CHAPTER EIGHT

Ortberg, John. *Soul Keeping Study Guide: Caring for the Most Important Part of You.* 2014. p. 42.

"10 Inspiring Eleanor Roosevelt Quotes." Unfoundation.org. Last modified August 27, 2018. https://unfoundation.org/blog/post/10-inspiring-eleanor-roosevelt-quotes/.

Bhasin, Hitesh. "4 Types Of Creativity." Marketing91. Last modified October 12, 2021. https://www.marketing91.com/4-types-of-creativity/.

"Definitions of Creativity." www.andyeklund.com. Accessed October 25, 2022. https://andyeklund.com/definitions-of-creativity.

"How Much Did Nike Pay for 'Just Do It'?" Vernacular. Last modified February 22, 2018. https://www.vernacular.co.nz/much-nike-pay-just.

"David Ogilvy: "Big Ideas Come from the Unconscious"." Brian John Spencer. Last modified June 8, 2013. https://brianjohnspencer.blogspot.com/2013/06/david-ogilvy-ideas-come-from-unconscious.html.

Goldman, Jason G. "Creativity: The Weird and Wonderful Art of Animals." BBCpage. Accessed October 25, 2022. https://www.bbc.com/future/article/20140723-are-we-the-only-creative-species.

"8 Animal Species Who Could Totally Rule The World If They Tried A Little Harder." Reader's Digest. Last modified August 4, 2021. https://www.rd.com/list/smartest-animals/.

## CHAPTER NINE

"A Quote from Pride and Prejudice." Goodreads | Meet Your Next Favorite Book. Accessed October 25, 2022. https://www.

goodreads.com/quotes/120154-there-is-a-stubbornness-about-me-that-never-can-bear.

Bryan, Rebecca. "Phelps hungry for more after 21st gold." Yahoo. Accessed October 25, 2022. https://www.yahoo.com/news/us-gymnast-biles-flies-high-serena-crashes-rio-023254873--oly.html.

"A Quote by Leonard Ravenhill." Goodreads | Meet Your Next Favorite Book. Accessed October 25, 2022. https://www.goodreads.com/quotes/111470-a-man-who-is-intimate-with-god-is-not-intimidated.

CHAPTER TEN

"A Quote by H.S. Crow." Goodreads | Meet Your Next Favorite Book. Accessed October 25, 2022. https://www.goodreads.com/quotes/9264957-creative-people-have-it-hard-there-is-always-something-trapped.

Rodriguez, Tori. "Writing Can Help Injuries Heal Faster." Scientific American. Last modified November 1, 2013. https://www.scientificamerican.com/article/writing-can-help-injuries-heal-faster/.

"Interactive Keynote Adam Grant at the 2017 SXSW Conference [Video]." SXSW. Last modified March 15, 2017. https://www.sxsw.com/news/2017/interactive-keynote-adam-grant-2017-sxsw-conference-video/.

"Steve Jobs Think different Crazy ones speech." YouTube. 1. February 7, 2018. https://www.youtube.com/watch?v=4f-cb8eu20SQ.

Cullum, Erin. "15 Facts About Sunny Anderson That Will Make You Love Her Even More." POPSUGAR Food. Last modified

August 14, 2016. https://www.popsugar.com/food/Sunny-Anderson-Fun-Facts-42208336.

Anderson, Sunny. "Sunny Anderson's Tribute To B. Smith." Food Network. Last modified October 7, 2020. https://www.foodnetwork.com/profiles/talent/sunny-anderson/sunny-anderson-tribute-to-b--smith.

"Billionaire Pastor Unveils $300 Million Temple of Solomon Church Replica in Brazil." The Christian Post. Last modified August 6, 2014. https://www.christianpost.com/news/billionaire-pastor-unveils-300-million-temple-of-solomon-church-replica-in-brazil.html.

Lambert, Kyle. "Kyle Lambert." Kyle Lambert - Illustrator / Movie Poster Artist. Accessed October 25, 2022. https://www.kylelambert.com/about/.

"Edwin H. Land Quote." Lib Quotes. Accessed October 25, 2022. https://libquotes.com/edwin-h-land/quote/lbz6h0k.

"From Depressed to Self Lovin' Millionaire with Libby Crow." Accessed October 25, 2022. https://rawbeauty.co/libby-crow/.

"The 20 Best Cindy Trimm Quotes." Book Subscription Box for Kids - Book Club for Ages 0-12. Accessed October 25, 2022. https://bookroo.com/quotes/cindy-trimm.

CHAPTER ELEVEN

Ott, Tim. "Bethany Hamilton." Biography. Last modified June 12, 2015. https://www.biography.com/athlete/bethany-hamilton/.

"Surfer Bethany Hamilton Talks Recovery and Faith, 13 Years After Shark Attack." TODAY.com. Last modified November 1, 2016. https://www.today.com/health/surfer-bethany-hamilton-talks-recovery-faith-13-years-after-shark-t104551.

"Resilience." Www.dictionary.com. Accessed October 25, 2022. https://www.dictionary.com/browse/resilience.

"How Resilience Helps You Cope With Challenges." Verywell Mind. Last modified January 27, 2009. https://verywellmind. com/what-is-resilience-2795059.

Management Training and Leadership Training – Online. Accessed October 25, 2022. https://www.mindtools.com/pages/article/ newCDV_90.html.

"About Us." Kind Design. Accessed October 25, 2022. https://www. kinddesign.co/pages/about-us/.

"Wonder: The Emotional Story Behind R.J. Palacio Book and Movie." Peoplemag. Last modified November 17, 2017. https:// people.com/movies/wonder-rj-palacio-story-behind-book/.

"A Quote by Mandy Hale." Goodreads | Meet Your Next Favorite Book. Accessed October 25, 2022. https://www.goodreads. com/quotes/1023321-growth-is-painful-change-is-painful-but-nothing-is-as.

"A Quote by George Bernard Shaw." Goodreads | Meet Your Next Favorite Book. Accessed October 25, 2022. https://www. goodreads.com/quotes/87185-progress-is-impossible-without-change-and-those-who-cannot-change.

*Mulan.* Directed by Niki Caro. 2020. Walt Disney Pictures, 2020. Film.

CHAPTER TWELVE

"Meet Our Founder: Alexandra Scott." Alex's Lemonade Stand Foundation for Childhood Cancer. Last modified August 3, 2022. https://www.alexslemonade.org/about/meet-alex.

Oldskoolbball. "Michael Jordan On Being Cut From High School

Varsity: "I Just Wasn't Good Enough."." Oldskoolbball.
Last modified April 7, 2020. https://oldskoolbball.com/michael-jordan-high-school-varsity/.

"MSN." MSN | Outlook, Office, Skype, Bing, Breaking News, and Latest Videos. Accessed October 25, 2022. https://www.msn.com/en-us/sports/nba/michael-jordans-secret-to-success-ive-missed-more-than-9000-shots-in-my-career-ive-lost-almost-300-games-ive-failed-over-and-over-and-over-again-in-my-life-and-that-is-why-i-succeed/ar-AAT9Rmv.

Covey, Stephen R. *The 7 Habits of Highly Effective People: Powerful Lessons in Personal Change.* New York: Simon & Schuster, 2013. 1.

*The Princess Diaries.* Directed by Garry Marshall. 2001. Walt Disney Pictures, 2001. Film.

DR. KIM ALLEN IS AN ACCOMPLISHED professional in Information Technology, Spiritual Leadership, and Education. With specialties in planning, professional development, adult education, and small group leadership, she develops and presents curricula, mentors women who need technical skills to return to the workplace, and assists other spiritual leaders in facilitating life-changing materials.

Dr. Allen received her Master's degree in Business Computer Information Systems Management and Doctorate of Theology while working full time, pastoring, raising a family, leading small groups, and mentoring students. In addition, through online education, Dr. Allen has provided curriculum resources worldwide.

Made in the USA
Monee, IL
29 April 2023

32481679R00111